How to Teach the Research Report

By David S. Dye, M.Ed.

For workshop / staff development information call
(562) 627-5662 or go to CreateBetterWriters.com.

Model Citizen Enterprises
Long Beach, CA 90808
CreateBetterWriters.com

ISBN: 978-1481958875

Table of Contents

Introduction

Writing a research report is one of the most dreaded assignments in all of school. It is difficult to teach, and it is difficult to complete. It involves a great deal of work for both the teachers and students. When students are assigned a research report, they know they are in for a long, difficult journey. Worst of all, many of the students will lack the skills, confidence or both which makes this a daily frustrating experience.

I've been teaching for more than twenty years, and I've never felt that I've had the perfect solution for teaching this assignment. It just seems so bizarre for me to give a 3-5 report when many of my students are barely writing essays. Therefore, just like everything else, I decided to break the research report down into its simplest form and build from the ground up.

One of the problems with teaching the research report is that it takes a long time to complete. Students will make mistakes and stumble clumsily through the project. They will not have a chance to learn from this process until the next report is given which is often a year later when their next teacher repeats this process.

There is a solution. What if the students can practice the research process multiple times on short assignments. This would allow them the opportunity to make mistakes, take chances, and develop a personal style before trying the longer assignment.

With this thought in mind I began teaching the one paragraph research report. Within two weeks, I was able to model the research process several times, give them guided practice, and have them try the report on their own. We next graduated to the five paragraph research report which took very little time. The students had already learned the hardest part – how to find and organize details on a specific main idea. Fortunately, I had this same group of students for a second year and was able to teach them the final step, the 3-5 page research report.

The important idea to remember when teaching the research report is to keep it as simple as possible. By making the process for writing the one paragraph research report the same the 3-5 page research report, the students didn't feel like they were doing anything different. Here is an overview of the process:

The goal here is to keep the students thinking in threes. For the paragraph, the students are going to look for three things: a beginning, middle, and end and write their paragraph around that. For the essay, they will find a beginning, middle, and end and base each paragraph on these. Finally, the student will find a beginning, middle, and end for their 3-5 page research report. Each of those main ideas will form the foundation for the three sections of their report. The students can follow this pattern into the ten page report and beyond. The longer the report, the more main ideas they will find, and each main idea will have a beginning, middle, and end. Below is a visual of this concept.

<u>Overview of the system (See Outline)</u>

Key Point: All reports have a beginning, middle, and end.

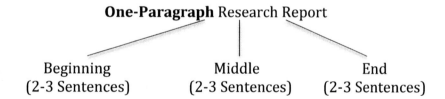

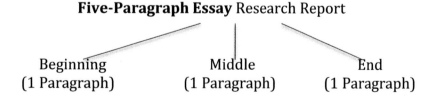

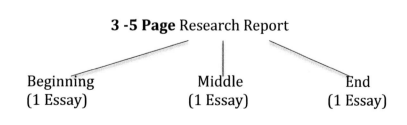

Outline for Each Section

After becoming comfortable with each section of this book, use these outlines as a handy reference while teaching.

One-Paragraph Research Report

1. Teach the paragraph paper setup.
2. Select a topic and gather three resources.
3. Get the students comfortable with the topic.
4. Take notes from resource #1.
5. Take notes from resource #2
6. Take notes from resource #3
7. Finish the prewriting by numbering the details and writing the one main idea of the paragraph.
8. Write the paragraph as a class. Model the difference between listing sentences and having the sentences flow together.
9. Edit, revise, and publish. Add the footnotes and bibliography.
10. Follow up ideas for the one-paragraph research report.

Five-Paragraph Research Report

1. Select a topic and gather three resources.
2. Note Taking: Have the students take out four (4) pieces of paper. Write "Main Idea #1," "Main Idea #2," and "Main Idea #3," respectively, on the first three and "Prewrite" in the center of the fourth page. *I will refer to each of these pages as Main Idea #1 Note Page, Main Idea #2 Note Page, Main Idea #3 Note Page, and the Research Report Prewrite.

3. Get comfortable with the topic. Have the students look through their three resources. Have them focus on finding three main ideas for their report by looking at the headings and pictures. These are great sources to help find your three main ideas for your report.

4. Find the three main ideas for your report from resource #1. Write possible main ideas on the Main Idea #1 Note Page. Once the students have listed several possible main ideas, have them select the three they like the most. Have them write these on the top of their Research Report Prewrite and their Main Idea Note Pages.

5. Take notes from resource #1 on Main Idea #1 Note Page.
   A. Write the citation information from this resource.
   B. Write possible details on the Main Idea #1 Note Page.
   C. From these notes, select the three details representing the beginning, middle, and end of the report. Write these three details on the Research Report Prewrite.
   D. Repeat Steps A, B and C for Main Idea #2. Use the Main Idea Note Page #2.
   E. Repeat Steps A, B and C for Main Idea #3. Use the Main Idea Note Page #3.

6. Take notes on resource #2.
   A. Take notes for Main Idea #1. Review the three details already found from resource #1.
   B. Find two or three details that expand on details already found from resource #1. You are just looking for details that will expand on these ideas.
   C. Select the two or three best details. Write them on the Research Report Prewrite.
   D. Repeat Steps A, B, and C for Main Idea #2. Use the Main Idea Note Page #2.
   E. Repeat Steps A, B, and C for Main Idea #3. Use the Main Idea Note Page #3.

7. Repeat the previous step for resource #3.

8. Organize your notes. Now that you have all the details you need for all three paragraphs, it's time to decide the best order for the facts to appear in the

paragraphs. For each main idea, number the details in the order that they will appear in the paragraphs.

9. Write the introduction. The thesis statement should give the central idea of the report with a general overview of the main ideas of the report.

10. Write the three body paragraphs.

11. Write the conclusion paragraph.

12. Make the endnotes and bibliography.

13. Conclusion: Edit, Revise, Final Draft, and Next Steps

Three- to Five-Page Research Report

1. Select a topic and gather at least three resources.
2. Set up your paper and find your report's main ideas.
   a. Set up your first paper for your bibliography and general notes for main ideas.
   b. Research and take notes until you have three or four main ideas. Write each main idea on the top of a sheet of paper.
   c. Finish your paper setup by putting "Beginning," "Middle," and "End" on each sheet of paper.
3. Take notes from resource #1. Find a few facts for the beginning, middle, and end of each of your topics. Be sure to write roman numeral #1 and the page number where the details were found next to all the details you find from this resource.
4. Take notes on resources #2, #3, and so on until you have enough details to write about all of your main ideas. Put roman numeral #2 next to the details from the second resource, roman numeral #3 next to the details found from the third resource, and so on for each resource you use. Be sure to put page numbers as well.

5. Write the introduction to the report. Include a thesis statement that gives the central idea of your report, and summarize the main ideas of the report.

6. Write the body of your report. Include an endnote in subscript[1] for any major detail or when you are quoting/citing someone's opinion.

7. Write the conclusion of your report. Summarize your thesis statement and review your main ideas.

8. Revise and edit your report.

9. Type and turn in your report.

Part I
The One-Paragraph Research Report

How many times will a student need to practice the research report until he/she has it mastered? Some might need a few tries, while others might need several tries each year until they finally master it. It is not realistic to expect teachers to give multiple research reports each year with the specific intent of teaching the research report. On the other hand, it seems unfair to expect students to be able to do a research report without being given the basic skills for completing the task. Nevertheless, by late middle school and into high school, teachers will assign research reports with the expectation that students will know how to complete the task.

In my academic career, I've been assigned dozens of research reports without specifically being taught the process for completing the task. I began each assignment with a complete lack of confidence. I struggled through the assignments and hoped for the best. I received little feedback on my finished work, usually receiving a B without any knowledge as to what I did right or wrong to deserve that grade. I now watch my own children going through middle and high school following the same process with the same feelings of anxiety.

There is a solution for this problem. Why not teach the research report writing process within a single paragraph? Within a week, a teacher can model all the steps required to write a research report and give the students opportunities to try it on their own. This will give students confidence going into larger assignments.

A great aspect about teaching the one-paragraph research report is that it gives the teachers an opportunity to reinforce the subjects they are already teaching. Just select a topic of study that the students are going to study anyway, and have them write one-paragraph research reports for those. Social studies and science lend themselves well to this process.

Overview

When I first tried this process, I was teaching fifth grade. I selected seven causes of the American Revolution as our topic for the mini research reports. For each topic, we had a section in our social studies book to use as a resource. Additionally, I had workbooks with summaries of the events for another resource. For a third resource, I copied one-page reports from the Internet and made copies for  the class. In this way, we had a variety of resources to use for our report.

We began our first topic by setting up our paper for a paragraph. This prewrite would be a place to begin organizing our information. Next, we read the book, found a beginning, middle, and end for the topic, and recorded them on our prewrite. We then read the worksheet and looked for two details that supported the beginning, middle, and end that we had already found in the book. Finally, we studied the Internet article and added two more details that supported the other details. Using these seven details, we wrote a topic sentence, completed the paragraph, added a closing sentence, and were finished. The entire process took two days.

I modeled this process a second time. As we completed a second paragraph as a class, I could see the light bulbs going on above the students' heads. They were getting it.

For the next two topics, I decided that I would begin the one-paragraph report with the students and allow them to finish it on their own. We found the beginning, middle, and end together, and I allowed the students to finish the rest in pairs.

The students were given even more independence for the final paragraphs. For the next paragraph, the students were allowed to do the entire process in pairs. They completed the next paragraph on their own as a practice test, and the last paragraph became their final exam.

This process took about three weeks. We did the research in class, and the paragraphs were written for homework. We would later follow these same steps while writing the five-paragraph research report for the Westward Movement. Although we were writing longer reports, it only took a week to practice before the students were independently writing their own papers. The one-paragraph research report had prepared them well, and I had already taught the five-paragraph essay, so the transition was almost effortless.

The Steps:

Step 1: Teach the paragraph paper setup.

If you use *How to Teach the Paragraph*, you have already taught your students one simple trick that will help them master the paragraph. We will be using this trick throughout the book as students learn to transition from paragraphs to essays to multiple page reports. It is a good idea to teach the paragraph first, as students who can write a strong paragraph going into this process will learn it more quickly and have a better chance for lifelong mastery.

Since a paragraph is about one main idea, the students need to make sure that their paragraphs stay focused on their one main idea. To do this, they will begin by setting up their papers for the paragraph. Model the steps below:

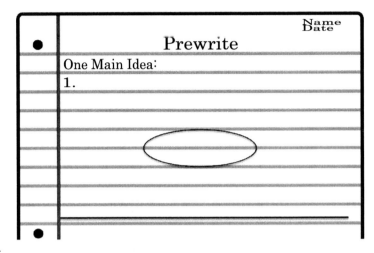

1. Have them put their names and "Prewrite" at the top of their papers.

2. Write "One Main Idea" on the first line with the #1 on the line below.

3. Make a cluster and draw a line through the middle of the paper.

*Ultimately, the students will be writing their paragraphs on the bottom half of the paper.

Step 2: Select a topic and gather resources.

What is the difference between a book report and a research report? This is the question I ask my students as we work through the research report. A book report is based on a single source. For a research report, students need to find information from multiple sources. This information is combined into one organized essay. Because our research report is only one paragraph, combining multiple sources can get a little tricky.

Picking Your Topic:

Since this report is just one paragraph long, you need to select a topic that has a narrow focus. A topic such as "The Causes of the American Revolution" would be too broad. Students would have a hard time keeping the topic focused on one paragraph. However, "The Boston Tea Party" is a topic that would have a clear beginning, middle and end.

Gather Resources

Since this is a one-paragraph introductory lesson, gather the three sources for the students. As they begin to master this skill, you can have them practice gathering the material on their own.

Try to keep the length of the resources to one or two pages. A couple of pages from a textbook, a worksheet from a workbook, and an article from the Internet work very well.

The main objective of the one-paragraph research report is to train the students to look for relevant details and ignore the irrelevant details. By using one- to two-page sources, the students will be able to see important and unimportant details more clearly. This will help them as they move on to larger resources, such as books.

Summary of Step 2

1. Select your topic. Be sure to choose a topic that has a narrow focus.
2. Use your textbook or a reliable source as your first resource.
3. Gather two more resources. One should be an Internet article, magazine, or video.

Whatever topic you're researching, there is likely to be a section in your textbook about it. Textbooks make a good first resource as they usually give a good overview of a topic without going into great detail. If your topic is not in a textbook, find a book that has a good overview of the subject. Finally, gather two more resources on your topic which will give you a total of three. Use an Internet article as one of your resources. This will also get them into the habit of using multiple types of resources. Other ideas for a third resource can be a video or magazine/newspaper article.

Example of Step 2:

Select a topic and gather resources.

1. My fifth grade class was studying the American Revolution. I chose to have the students write their first research report on the French and Indian War.

2. Our social studies book gave a good two-page overview of the topic. We used that as our first resource.

3. I had an American Revolution workbook that had a short story about the French and Indian War. I made copies and used this as our second resource.

4. Finally, I found a nice half-page article at SocialStudiesForKids.com. I printed out the article and made copies for the students.

Step 3: Get the students comfortable with the topic.

When students do a larger research report, they won't start note taking right away. They will spend some time becoming familiar with the topic. As they do this, they should start looking for main ideas and themes that emerge. The students will simulate this by taking some time to review their topic.

1. Give the students a few minutes to read the first resource. They don't need to finish reading the entire text. Let them know that they will be asked to share details when finished.

2. Give the students a couple of minutes to read the second source. Tell them to look for details that are similar to the first source. Ask, "Did you notice any of the same details? Did you notice any additional facts that expanded on details from the first source?"

3. Repeat this procedure for the third source. If you are using a video for the third source, you can skip this step.

Example of Step 3: Get the students comfortable with the topic.

1. I gave the students three minutes to scan the textbook looking for facts about the French and Indian War. I gave raffle tickets as rewards for students who could give me details about what was in the text. Students offered information such as: George

Washington was involved; the French were fighting the British; the British won; American Indians fought on both sides.

Just with the details the class shared from memory, we could have written the paragraph right then. We discussed why we were **not** going to write the paragraph right now. If we did, it would become a book report rather than a research report.

2. The students were given two more minutes to scan the second source. They were asked to look for similar details as the first source. Again, raffle tickets were given to students who could identify details that were similar to the first resource.

3. The students were given two more minutes to look through the article from the Internet. We quickly reviewed the similar details and were ready to move on to Step 3.

Step 4: Take Notes - Resource #1.

Keep in mind that the students only get one paragraph to write their report. That's five to seven sentences. This leads to two important details:
1. The students cannot go into much detail about the topic. Only the most important facts can go into the paragraph.
2. Since the students need to combine facts from three resources, they cannot find too many facts from one resource. That means that they can only find two or three facts from each resource.

Consequently, you are going to use the first resource to give a complete overview of the topic. Their goal for the first resource is to find the beginning, middle, and end of the topic.

Therefore, <u>have them begin by writing B, M, and E around their cluster. Also, have them write #1 next to the B, M, and E to</u> indicate that this information comes from their first resource. This will come in handy if you want to have your students cite their source.

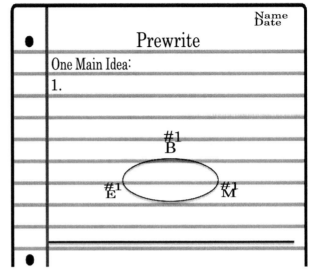

Next, read the first resource as a class. Let them know that their goal is to just find the beginning, middle, and end of the topic. After reading through the resource, have the students suggest a beginning, middle, and end. After coming to a final decision, the students will write the beginning, middle, and end <u>in their own words</u> on their paper.

Regarding the note taking, it is especially important that the students begin to learn how to put their notes into their own words. If they copy from the text into their notes, and they copy from their notes into their report, they are still plagiarizing. I've had many parents and students insist that they did not copy their report. They insist that they wrote their reports using their notes. After further investigation, they come to realize that the giant, five-syllable words in their notes did, in fact, come from the book.

Example of Step 4: Take Notes - Resource #1.

I modeled this step for the students using a model of a piece of paper, complete with margin lines burned onto a plastic overhead transparency. I've also done this step using a large piece of butcher paper, and I've modeled this step on a piece of paper underneath a document camera.

I wrote the B, M, and E with the #1 next to each on the paper, directing the students to copy it exactly where I put them. Before moving on, I checked that the students had done it correctly.

Next, we read the text together. Before beginning, we talked about the meaning of the words "relevant" and "irrelevant." As we read, we would stop at various sentences to discuss relevant and irrelevant details. For example, we decided that, considering that we only had one paragraph, adding George Washington's involvement was irrelevant. However, the factors that started the war, such as the French and British both claiming the land in the Ohio River Valley, were relevant.

After reading, I let the students work in pairs. Their job was to come up with a beginning, middle, and end to the French and Indian War. I had an idea in mind already for the three, so I was looking for the students whose answers were closest to my own. After selecting groups to share their results,

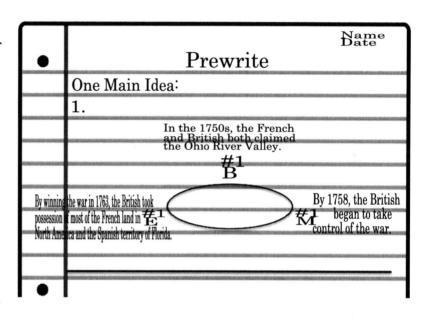

it didn't take long to generate the three details. We then wrote them on our notes.

Step 5: Take Notes - Resource #2.

The goal for this step is to find details that will either support the beginning, middle, and end or fill in the timeline between the three events. If you look at my example about the French and Indian War, you will notice that our details from resource #2 will do both.

Remember, the students can only find two facts from this resource, which will bring their notes up to five details. Therefore, as you read the resource as a class, look for the details that fill in the timeline or add important facts to the beginning, middle, and end. Have the students point out similar details from the first resource and see if there is anything new to add. When you've done this, add the two details to your prewrite. Be sure to put a #2 next to these details to note that these details came from the second resource. Again, this will come in handy if you choose to start adding footnotes to the report.

Example of Step 5: Take Notes - Resource #2

We jumped straight from the first resource to the second, so there was no need to review the three main ideas from resource #1. If we had started this step at a later date, we would have begun with a review of the beginning, middle, and end.

We began by looking at the first fact we found: in the 1750s, the French and British both claimed the Ohio River Valley. We then looked at the second fact: by 1758, the British began to take control of the war. It wasn't hard to see that there were missing details between the beginning and middle of the report. Therefore, our goal was to look for details that would bridged the gap between the beginning and middle or expanded on one of the two.

As we began to read, we noticed that the first few paragraphs had nothing to do with bridging the gap between our beginning and middle facts. The students quickly noticed that they could scan the first few paragraphs because they were just looking for a fact that explained what happened after the war began. Then they found it. Resource #2 described how the British struggled early in the war because the French and their American Indian allies fought using guerilla tactics where the British expected to fight in

open fields. This became our detail from this source.

After writing the fact on our prewrite, some students pointed out that that detail was also in resource #1. We were able to discuss that a research report is more

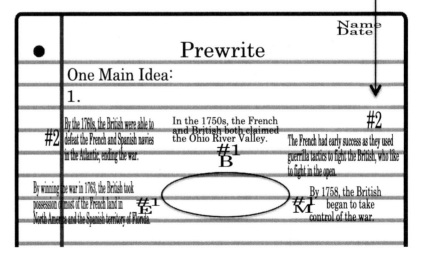

20

reliable than a book report because several sources will confirm that certain details are true. By citing that this detail comes from resource #2, it adds credibility to our report.

Finally, we looked for a detail that would bridge the gap between the middle and end facts from resource #1. Since our last detail from the first resource described what the British gained from the war, we thought a detail about how the fighting ended would be appropriate. By now, the students knew that they could scan the resource searching for this fact. They found it when they saw that the British navy was able to defeat both France and Spain in Europe and their territories in the Atlantic Ocean. This was the fact that went on their prewrite.

Step 6: Take Notes - Resource #3.

By the time the students get to resource #3, they probably have enough facts to write their paragraph. The goal for this resource can be:

1. Find details that fill any gaps in our report. If the beginning, middle, or end is not fully developed, this would be the time to find a detail to support it.
2. Find a good quote that might add to the paragraph. If the report is about John Paul Jones, the students might add the quote "I have not yet begun to fight!" to their notes.
3. Find a colorful detail that might expand on one of the main ideas of the report. In a report on the Boston Massacre, we read that the colonists had tarred and feathered British tax collectors, showing that there was a history of violence from the colonists. While this may not be a relevant detail, it wouldn't hurt to add a colorful side note to the paragraph.

As the students write their notes from this resource, be sure to have them label their details with #3. This will allow them to identify where they found these facts if you decide to make footnotes.

Example of Step 6: Take Notes - Resource #3.

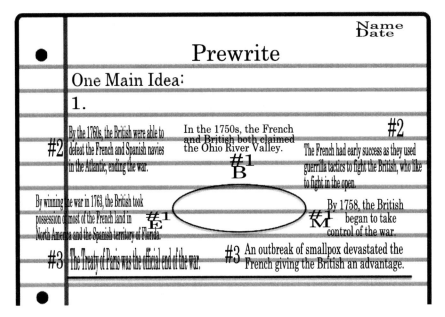

By the time we got to resource #3, we had found most of the facts needed for the paragraph. Therefore, we really only needed to see if there was a detail that would expand on what we had already found. Again, we scanned the text, searching only for details that added to what we already had. The only new information was that the Treaty of Paris was the official end to the war. We added this detail to our notes with the #3 next to it. We did find a good anecdote about smallpox hurting the French and American Indians during the war. We wrote it down in case we could fit it in the paragraph.

Step 7: Finish the prewrite.

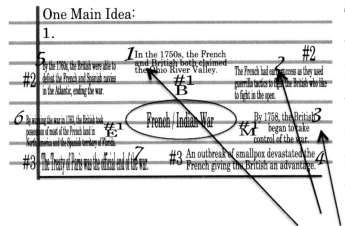

The students now have everything they need to write their paragraphs. However, it helps them organize their paragraph if they put their details in order and write the main idea of the paragraph on the top of their prewrite.

Have the students look at their notes. Number the details in the order that they should be placed in their paragraphs. The arrows above point to the first three of the seven details. Next, have the students write a one-sentence summary of their topic below "One Main Idea" next to the #1 on their prewrite. The students tend to overthink this step. They just need to simply state the main idea of the report. For fifth graders, it may be as easy as "The Boston Tea Party was a cause of the American Revolution." Older students can make it more intelligent by expanding on the same idea: "As colonists grew more tired of British taxation without representation, a late-night raid in Boston Harbor would further add tensions to an ever increasing conflict."

Example of Step 7: Finish the prewrite.

In our examples on the previous page, notice how all of our details are scrambled on the paper. As a class, we talked about the order that the sentences should appear in the paragraph. Obviously, the beginning would go first. However, did we find another fact that might precede this? It didn't take much effort to see the natural order for the details of the report.

With the order of the details fresh in our minds, we then discussed the main idea of the report. In one sentence, the students are required to summarize the main idea of the paragraph and write it under "One Main Idea" on their prewriting.

Practice this by having the students write a sentence that they think summarizes the main idea of the report. To help them do this, they can ask, "What is our reader going to learn from this report?" Ask the students to share what they have written. Select one of the main

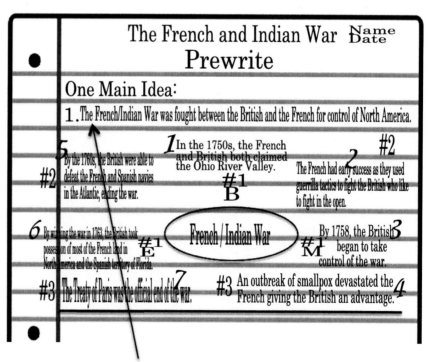

idea sentences or have one prewritten, and have the class write it on their prewrite.

Step 8: Write the paragraph.

This should actually be the easiest part of the report. The hard work is done. We have all the facts we need, and they are labeled in the correct order in which they should appear in the paragraph. We even wrote the one main idea which can serve as our topic sentence. There's nothing left to do except write it out.

Point out to the students that the one main idea can act as their topic sentence. Let the more advanced students try to be more creative. However, most students can simply rewrite what was written on their prewrite.

The French and Indian War
Prewrite

Name
Date

One Main Idea:

1. The French/Indian War was fought between the British and the French for control of North America.

1 In the 1750s, the French and British both claimed the Ohio River Valley. *#1 B*

#2 By the 1760s, the British were able to defeat the French and Spanish navies in the Atlantic, ending the war.

2 #2 The French had early success as they used guerrilla tactics to fight the British who like to fight in the open.

French / Indian War

A By winning the war in 1763, the British took possession of most of the French land in North America and the Spanish territory of Florida. *#1 B*

#1 M By 1758, the British began to take control of the war. *3*

#3 The Treaty of Paris was the official end of the war. *7*

#3 An outbreak of smallpox devastated the French giving the British an advantage. *4*

The French and Indian War was fought between the British and the French for control of North America. It began in the 1750's when the French and British both claimed the land in the Ohio River Valley. As war broke out, the French had early success as they used guerrilla tactics to fight while the British were used to fighting in the open. By 1758, the British began to take control of the war. The fighting then transitioned to Europe, and the British were able to beat the French and Spanish, who had joined the French later in the war. The Treaty of Paris was signed in 1763 officially ending the war. By winning the war, the British took control of the French land in North America and gained the Spanish territory of Florida from Spain. Because of the French and Indian War, the British were now the main power in North America.

When it comes to writing the body of the report, many students want to copy the details straight from their prewriting. The problem with this is that their paragraph ends up sounding like a grocery list rather than a smooth, flowing report.

Write the paragraph together. One way to point out the need for smooth transitions between sentences is to read the prewrite to the students in the order you have already created. It will probably sound choppy and unpolished. (You will see a sample of this on the next page.) Then, as you write the paragraph together, you can point out how using pronouns to tie ideas together helps create a flow. Adding phrases of changing words can also help the paragraph become smoother.

> The French and Indian War was fought between the British and the French for control of North America. In the 1750's, the French and British both claimed the Ohio River Valley. The French had early success as they used guerrilla tactics to fight the British who like the fight in the open. By 1758, the British began to take control of the war. An outbreak of smallpox devistated the French giving the British an advantage. By 1760's, the British were able to defeat the French and Spanish navies in the Atlantic ending the war. By winning the war in 1763, the British took possession of most of the French land in North America and the Spanish territory in Florida. The Treaty of Paris was the official end of the war.

Some students will try copying the paragraph straight from their notes. You can see in this paragraph to the left that the sentences do not flow together. Because we found the details for our notes as a class, these sentences are fairly polished. However, when the students try this on their own, the problem will be much more obvious.

The paragraph below is the paragraph with the smooth transitions. There were several issues within the paragraph that we used to demonstrate how a paragraph should flow together.

1. We used phrases such as "It began in..." and "As war broke out..." to create a transition between sentences.

2. We removed detail #4 from our prewriting completely as it didn't seem to fit the context of the paragraph. It is important to let the students know that it is acceptable to

> The French and Indian War was fought between the British and the French for control of North America. It began in the 1750's when the French and British both claimed the land in the Ohio River Valley. As war broke out, the French had early success as they used guerrilla tactics to fight while the British were used to fighting in the open. By 1758, the British began to take control of the war. The fighting then transitioned to Europe, and the British were able to beat the French and Spanish, who had joined the French later in the war. The Treaty of Paris was signed in 1763, officially ending the war. By winning the war, the British took control of the French land in North America and gained the Spanish territory of Florida from Spain. Because of the French and Indian War, the British were now the main power in North America.

> The French and Indian War was fought between the British and the French for control of North America. It began in the 1750's when the French and British both claimed the land in the Ohio River Valley. As war broke out, the French had early success as they used guerrilla tactics to fight while the British were used to fighting in the open. By 1758, the British began to take control of the war. The fighting then transitioned to Europe, and the British were able to beat the French and Spanish, who had joined the French later in the war. The Treaty of Paris was signed in 1763, officially ending the war. By winning the war, the British took control of the French land in North America and gained the Spanish territory of Florida from Spain. Because of the French and Indian War, the British were now the main power in North America.

add or remove details as they write. We also removed the part in detail #5 about the navies as it also didn't seem to fit the flow of the paragraph.

3. As we wrote, we felt that detail #7 fit better before detail #6. Therefore, we identified that the Treaty of Paris ended the war and then wrote about the result of the war.

4. We added a closing sentence. Since the French and Indian War had a major consequence, we decided to end the paragraph with that.

Ultimately, if this paragraph is not smooth and polished, I'm not that concerned. The entire point of this process is learning how to collect and organize details for research papers. In most cases, students will do research reports on topics that are completely unfamiliar to them. As they get better at the research aspect, the quality of the writing will improve as well.

Step 9: Write the final draft, footnotes, and bibliography.

There are many ways to revise, edit, and publish a final draft. However you choose to do it, the students should have a clean report free from errors.

Concerning footnotes or endnotes, at this point in the research paper process, I don't spend a lot of time with this step. For the one-paragraph research report, my main concern is collecting and organizing relevant facts that stay focused on the topic. As I move onto the five-paragraph research report, I will go over this in more detail.

For now, I simply want to give the students a brief overview of footnotes. Therefore, I didn't make them write page numbers for where the facts were found as would be done with a formal research report. We didn't record publisher information or any other details. As a result, our footnotes will just have the name of the book used to find the fact.

After the students write their final drafts, have them select three sentences, one sentence from each of the three resources used to create the prewrite. Have them put a 1, 2, or 3 at the end of the sentences. The 1 will correspond to the sentence that comes from the first resource. The 2 and 3 will go next to sentences that came

> The French and Indian War was fought between the British and the French for control of North America. It began in the 1750's when the French and British both claimed the land in the Ohio River Valley. As war broke out, the French had early success as they used guerrilla tactics to fight while the British were used to fighting in the open.[2] By 1758, the British began to take control of the war. The fighting then transitioned to Europe, and the British were able to beat the French and Spanish, who had joined the French later in the war. The Treaty of Paris was signed in 1763 officially ending the war.[3] By winning the war, the British took control of the French land in North America and gained the Spanish territory of Florida from Spain.[1] Because of the French and Indian War, the British were now the main power in North America.

from the second and third resources. To do this, they need to use their prewrite to see where each detail was found. Since each sentence in the report corresponds to a detail from their prewrite, they should be able to tell which sentence gets the 1, 2, or 3. See the example above.

For the one-paragraph research report, I just combined the footnotes with the bibliography. For older students, you can make it more formal if you like. For this example, I just have them write the title "Bibliography" in the center of their papers below their final draft. Next, they write the title of the book or resource and the author. Be sure that the numbers from the paragraph match the numbers of the resources in the bibliography.

Sample of Finished Product:

Below is a sample of the final prewrite with the rough draft and the final draft of the report.

The French and Indian War
Prewrite

One Main Idea:

1. The French/Indian War was fought between the British and the French for control of North America.

In the 1750s, the French and British both claimed the Ohio River Valley.

The French had early success as they used guerrilla tactics to fight the British who like to fight in the open.

By the 1760s, the British were able to defeat the French and Spanish navies in the Atlantic, ending the war.

French / Indian War

By 1758, the British began to take control of the war.

By winning the war in 1763, the British took control of most of the French land in North America and the Spanish territory of Florida.

The Treaty of Paris was the official end of the war.

An outbreak of smallpox devastated the French giving the British an advantage.

The French and Indian War was fought between the British and the French for control of North America. It began in the 1750's when the French and British both claimed the land in the Ohio River Valley. As war broke out, the French had early success as they used guerrilla tactics to fight while the British were used to fighting in the open. By 1758, the British began to take control of the war. The fighting then transitioned to Europe, and the British were able to beat the French and Spanish, who had joined the French later in the war. The Treaty of Paris was signed in 1763 officially ending the war. By winning the war, the British took control of the French land in North America and gained the Spanish territory of Florida from Spain. Because of the French and Indian War, the British were now the main power in North America.

The French and Indian War

The French and Indian War was fought between the British and the French for control of North America. It began in the 1750's when the French and British both claimed the land in the Ohio River Valley. As war broke out, the French had early success as they used guerrilla tactics to fight while the British were used to fighting in the open. By 1758, the British began to take control of the war. The fighting then transitioned to Europe, and the British were able to beat the French and Spanish, who had joined the French later in the war. The Treaty of Paris was signed in 1763 officially ending the war. By winning the war, the British took control of the French land in North America and gained the Spanish territory of Florida from Spain. Because of the French and Indian War, the British were now the main power in North America.

Bibliography

1. Textbook: *Reflections: United States History - Making a New Nation*
2. Thompson, Eric. *Stories of the American Revolution*
3. http://www.SocialStudiesForKids.com//articles/ushistory/frenchandindianwar1.htm

Step 10 – Follow up.

Depending on the ability level of your students, you may need to model the one-paragraph research report a few times before the students are ready to try it on their own. Middle school students may only need to see it once, while elementary school students may need several examples before they are ready for independent practice.

Whatever you decide, there is a sample lesson that I did with my fifth-grade students (see next page). These students have a variety of backgrounds and ability levels. By completing the seven paragraphs from this lesson, beginning with me modeling the process and gradually giving the students more responsibility until they could do it on their own, the students were highly successful.

The worksheet to the right (also in the appendix) shows how I planned the seven paragraphs out ahead of time. I listed the seven topics and collected two sources for each. I required them to find the third source on their own so they could practice looking for supporting details. As described earlier in this section, we completed the French and Indian War together. For each new paragraph, I did less and less with them until they were doing the last two paragrpahs on their own.

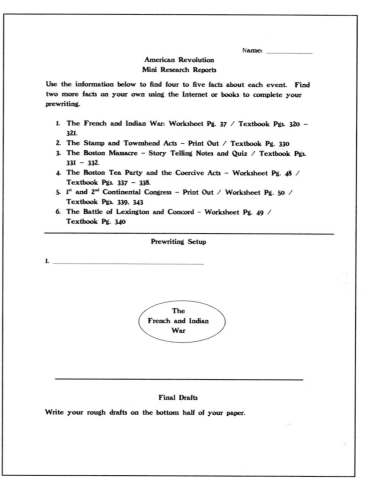

For example, we did a second report about the Stamp and Townsend Acts by finding the details from the first resource together. Then I allowed them to work in groups to find the facts for the second and third resources. For the third and fourth reports, I allowed the students to work in pairs. I brought the class together several times to discuss key issues as they worked. What facts did you find relevant? What were your beginning, middle, and end? What was your one main idea? Also, by pairing a high-level student with a low-level one, there was effective peer tutoring occurring in the class.

I was going to have them do a third report in pairs, but they insisted that they were ready to try it on their own...and they were. Most of the reports would have been excellent for middle school students. Considering that they were only fifth graders, the lesson could not have gone better.

The entire process took about two and a half weeks. Often, the students did rough drafts at home. When they worked on their own, they only needed about an hour of class time for the research. During this time, I made small groups with the struggling students. All things considered, a 75 percent success rate for a class of thirty-two students on such a difficult assignment is very impressive.

The best part of this entire experience is that the students are now very well prepared for larger essays. They've learned the hardest part of research report writing. They know how to find key details and organize them into paragraphs. Furthermore, since the class already knows how to write the five-paragraph essay, all we needed to do to turn this into a five-paragraph research report was to write an introduction and conclusion paragraph. The students selected three of their paragraphs from the American Revolution assignment, added the introduction and conclusion, and presto, they had a five-paragraph research report.

In the next section, you will see how to write the five paragraph research report. However, most of the "heavy lifting" is over. Now that your students can write a small research report, the transition to the larger report will be less difficult.

More Samples of Follow-Up Work

The next year, my sixth-grade students were studying Mesopotamia, so I had them do the one-paragraph research report with three major leaders: Sargon, Hammurabi, and Nebuchadnezzar. To the right is a sample of one showing a typed final draft with a figure of each leader standing on the paragraph taped to a rock figurine. The other images on the next page show the same final draft for

Hammurabi and Nebuchadnezzar. Finally, there is a picture of all three figures hanging in my classroom.

Hammurabi's Code

Hammurabi was the ruler of Babylon who created a "code" of laws. Hammurabi united Sumer and Akkad to create one big Mesopotamian empire. He combined laws from all his conquered territories and made one "code" consisting of 282 laws. This "code" became the legacy of Hammurabi because he was the first to write them all out on stone. The code consists of many laws that considered the saying "an eye for an eye." For example, if a man punched out the teeth of his equal, his teeth would be knocked out as well. Hammurabi, the ruthless king, is famous for the "code" of laws he had created.

Part II
The Five-Paragraph Research Report

In this section, it is assumed that the students have learned to complete the one-paragraph research report and that they have a general knowledge of essay writing. If you are beginning your instruction with the five-paragraph research report, you will want to go back and review the previous sections if you find anything confusing in the directions of this section.

When the students learned how to complete the one-paragraph research report, they learned to complete the following procedure:

1. Set up their paper for organizing their notes.
2. Read about their topic until they discovered a beginning, middle, and end or found three strong main ideas.
3. Take notes only on details that were relevant to the three main ideas.
4. Organize the notes.
5. Write their rough draft.

Basically, the students are going to do the exact same thing for the five-paragraph research report. If they were successful with the one-paragraph report, they will find the five-paragraph report easy. The only difference between the two is that it will take a little more time as they will do each step in a little more detail.

Step 1: Select a topic and gather three resources.

All my experiences with research report writing, from the time I was in third grade and beyond, began the same way. My teachers gave me a topic, told me to write a report about it, and told me to turn it in at a certain time. Like the proverbial father teaching his son to swim by throwing him in the lake, I was left alone to figure out how to do the report on my own. In most cases, my parents helped me find the main details, helped me organize them, and left me to copy the final draft from their notes.

By high school, I'd seen my parents do my research reports enough times that I was able to muddle through the projects. However, I was never really confident that I was doing them correctly. This is why I like to introduce the five paragraph research report by completing one together in class. This will show the students that the process isn't as difficult as they might think, will give them confidence as they work through the project, and will lower their anxiety when you give them a report to do on their own.

Basically, when you model this process, you will begin by selecting a subject from your curriculum. Gather three resources that can serve as the text to supply the details for your report. It would be a great idea to have at least one primary source, as students should be aware of the differences between primary and secondary sources.

Example of Step 1: Select a topic and gather three resources.

My sixth-grade students wrote a five paragraph research report about ancient Egypt. An entire chapter in our social studies book was devoted to this topic. I knew ahead of time that the three main ideas would be the Old Kingdom, the Middle Kingdom, and the New Kingdom. These would serve as the outline from our first resource. Next, it was easy to find a workbook from a teacher's supply store that had short articles on the three kingdoms of ancient Egypt. This would be our second resource. Finally, there are some excellent videos that take students on a tour of ancient Egypt giving examples of firsthand accounts about the life of the early Egyptians. This would serve as an excellent primary source.

Summary of Step 1

1. Select your topic.

2. Select three main ideas that would make good topics for the report.

3. Gather three resources for your report. Use textbooks, library books, and Internet articles.

Step 2: Set up four pieces of paper for note taking, or use the worksheets.

Most teachers I know swear by the note cards for research reports. My wife uses them in her classroom, all my children's teachers have used them, and most of my teacher friends use them. From personal experience with my own reports and when I've used note cards with my students, I find them clumsy. I find that I spend a great deal of time searching through and organizing my cards, which, for me, seriously slows the writing process.

I've found that I can organize my information into topics just as well by putting all my details from a resource on one page (one, two or three pages for longer research reports). I will show you this method. However, if you are devoted to the note cards, I'm sure you will see how you can complete these steps using that method.

Two options: At this point, you need to decide if you are going to have students set up their own papers for note taking or use the worksheets provided in the appendices. I like to make my students set up their own papers because it is more like a natural research report that they will get in high school or college. However, I have had struggling students who need to use worksheets to guide them through the steps. If you choose to have the students set up their own papers, you can make overheads of the worksheets and have them set up their papers using the worksheets as a model.

The image to the right is a copy of what the final prewrite will look like after the students have collected all of their information. You will see samples later in the chapter of what the student-made copy of this worksheet looks like.

The images on the next page are the front and back of the first worksheet (there are three total) where the students will begin organizing the main ideas of their report and where they will begin writing down possible details to support these main ideas. Again, you will see samples of student-made versions of this paper

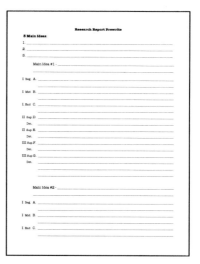

Worksheet for the final prewrite of the report

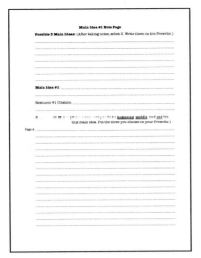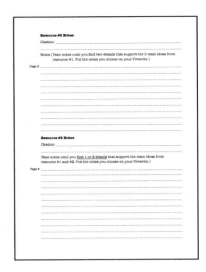

Front and back of the first of three worksheets where students will organize
their main ideas and begin writing supporting details for these main ideas.

If you are going to have the students set up their own papers for the prewrite and
note taking, here are the directions:

Begin by having the students take out four pieces of paper, one for each of the three
main ideas they will find and one for the final outline of the report, which I will call
the Prewrite. The students will write "Main Idea #1 Note Page," "Main Idea #2 Note
Page," and "Main Idea #3 Note Page" on the top of the first three papers, and
"Prewrite" on the top of the fourth.

Main Idea #1 Note Page is going to be the
students' primary paper for recording
bibliographical information and preparing the
students for the three main ideas of the report.
Therefore, the students will not only have
notes for the first main idea, they will have the
resource citations and notes for the three
overall main ideas of the report.

The text that the students need to copy
is in bold. The lines in between represent
the space they will need to leave for their notes.

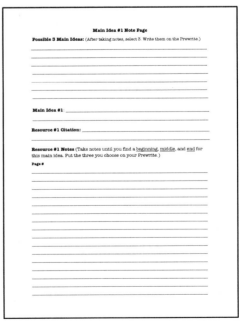

Model for students to use when
setting up their prewrite

36

The next paragraph will further explain this page. "Possible 3 Main Ideas" is where they will make a list of possible main ideas for their report. Next, the students will skip about seven lines and write "Main Idea #1:" followed by "Resource #1 Citation" and "Resource #1 Notes:" In the margin, have the students write "Page #."

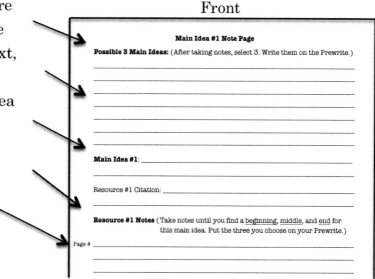

Front

Main Idea #1 Note Page

Possible 3 Main Ideas: (After taking notes, select 3. Write them on the Prewrite.)

_____
_____
_____
_____
_____
_____

Main Idea #1: _____
_____

Resource #1 Citation: _____
_____

Resource #1 Notes (Take notes until you find a <u>beginning</u>, <u>middle</u>, and <u>end</u> for this main idea. Put the three you choose on your Prewrite.)

Page # _____
_____
_____

On the back, have the students write "Resource #2 Notes" followed by "Citation" on the line below. On the next line, the students will write "Notes" with "Page #" in the margin. Finally, about half way down the page, the students will write "Resource #3 Notes," "Citation," and "Notes." Finally, they will write "Page #" in the margin.

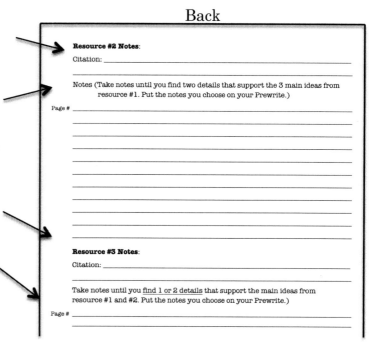

Back

Resource #2 Notes:

Citation: _____
_____

Notes (Take notes until you find two details that support the 3 main ideas from resource #1. Put the notes you choose on your Prewrite.)

Page # _____
_____
_____
_____
_____
_____
_____
_____

Resource #3 Notes:

Citation: _____

Take notes until you <u>find 1 or 2 details</u> that support the main ideas from resource #1 and #2. Put the notes you choose on your Prewrite.)

Page # _____
_____

The paper setup for the second and third pages is less complicated. On the next sheet, have the students write "Main Idea #2 Note Page," followed by "Main Idea #2:," and "Resource #1." On the back of the paper, have the students write "Resource #2" on the top line and "Resource #3" about half way down the paper.

Front

Back

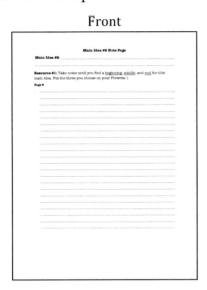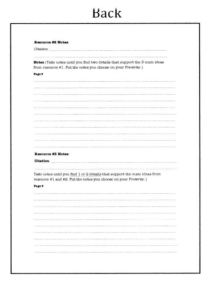

Repeat this process for the third sheet. Have the students write "Main Idea #3 Note Page," followed by "Main Idea #3:" and "Resource #1." On the back of the paper, have the students write "Resource #2" on the top line and "Resource #3" about half way down the paper.

The final step in the paper setup phase is to have the students set up their outline for the final report. This is the page where they will write the final notes that will become their report. If the students have been using the process from *How to Teach the Five Paragraph Essay*, they will find this very familiar.

Begin by having the students write "Research Report Prewrite" in the top center of the paper. Next, have them write "3 Main Ideas" followed by a "1." "2." and "3." on the lines below.

Below the three numbers, have the students write "Main Idea #1." From this point the students will skip lines as they write A through G. You might notice that the worksheet has "I Beg." "I Mid." and "I End" in the margins. I will go into more detail on that later. For now, all students need are the letters to represent the details for their reports.

Repeat this process for "Main Idea #2." And "Main Idea #3" using both sides of the paper.

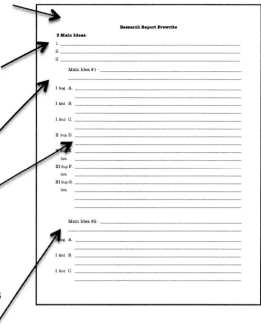

Filling in the Citation Information from Your Three Resources:

The paper setup is a good time to list the citations from the resources that will be used in the report. Main Idea #1 Note Page is now set up to receive this information.

The box below shows the information the students will need for each citation. Not all the information in the box will be available, so have the students put whatever information is available on their papers.

Citation

1. Author of resource
2. Book, magazine, Internet site, or title of resource such as CD or movie title.
3. Article title or chapter (if relevant).
4. City of publication (list only the first city).
5. Publisher and year of publication
6. Edition of the publication (if any).
- Videos, Internet articles, and other sources may not list some of this information. Simply list what you can find.

The example to the right shows how the students can document the citation. Once they have written the citation on their paper, they will not need to write it again until the final draft.

Main Idea #1: _____

_____

Resource #1 Citation: Reflections: Ancient Civilizations (Textbook); Chapter 4, Orlando, Harcourt, 2007

Resource #1 Notes (Take notes until you find a beginning, middle, and end for this main idea. Put the three you choose on your Prewrite.)

Page # _____

Students using note cards need to make a card with this citation and write the title of the resource on each card. They constantly forget to label each card, so this becomes a bigger time waster later as they repeatedly search for this information.

Step 3: Getting comfortable with your topic.

For most research reports, it would not be wise to jump into note taking before becoming familiar with the topic. The students should read about the topic, look at pictures, and especially start looking for themes or main ideas that continually jump out at them. My students, from writing paragraphs and essays all year, have become accustomed to looking for three main ideas as they scan a topic. This is a good habit to start when reviewing a topic.

To begin getting the students comfortable with the topic, give the students a few minutes to scan through the resources you've collected. Have them make a list of the following information:

1. What are some common themes that you notice in all the resources?
2. Do you notice any main ideas that would make good topics for the report? (Chapter titles and headings are good places to find these.)
3. Are there major events or famous people that come up?

Example of Step 3: Getting comfortable with your topic.

When my sixth-grade students reviewed resource #1, the chapter from our textbook, they saw that the chapter was divided into three lessons: the Old Kingdom, the Middle Kingdom, and the New Kingdom. Several pointed out that these would make a great beginning, middle, and end to our report. Other details that were noted were that pyramids were mainly built in the old kingdom, each period ended with the Egyptian society falling into chaos, and each kingdom had strong rulers. All of these would serve as good building blocks as we began to search for relevant details about our topic.

Step 4: Find your three main ideas from resource #1.

The goal for this step is for the students to formulate three main ideas for their topic. They can search for a beginning, middle, and end or three related main ideas for their topic. For a research report about ancient India, one of my classes came up with religion (Hinduism and Buddhism), daily life, and major empires. This didn't follow the beginning, middle, end format as other topics did, but still served as a good start for our report.

As the students read through resource #1, have them make a list of possible main ideas for their report on Main Idea Note Page #1. They should be looking for major themes or details that can tell a story. Keep taking notes until three main ideas appear such as a beginning, middle, and end.

Main Idea #1 Note Page

Possible 3 Main Ideas: (After taking notes, select 3. Write them on the Prewrite.)

_____
_____
_____
_____
_____
_____
_____

Main Idea #1: _____
_____

Resource #1 Citation: _____
_____

Resource #1 Notes (Take notes until you find a beginning, middle, and end for this main idea. Put the three you choose on your Prewrite.)

Page # _____

To the right is an image of a project we did as a class on ancient Egypt. As we read though our first resource, we found several topics that would have made great main ideas. Hint: The chapter titles and headings are great sources for main idea topics. With a little hint from you, the students will pick up on this in a hurry. While

> *Main Idea #1 Note Page*
>
> *Possible Main Ideas:*
> 1. *The Old Kingdom*
> 2. *Pyramids*
> 3. *Tomb / Afterlife*
> 4. *The Middle Kingdom*
> 5. *Famous Pharaohs*
> 6. *Social Life*
> 7. *Egyptian Gods*
> 8. *New Kingdom*
>
> *Main Idea #1:*

writing our reports, as the students were searching for possible main ideas, I would direct them to a chapter title and think out loud, "I wonder if 'The Old Kingdom' would make a good main idea for my essay?" When I did this, many of their eyes lit up, and immediately fingers were flashing through the pages looking for more chapter titles.

Use the list you generated and select three main ideas that work well together. Once you have found these three main ideas, have the students write them on their Research Report Prewrite.

Research Report Prewrite

3 Main Ideas:
1. Egypt's great dynasties began around 3100 BC during the Old Kingdom. (Beginning)
2. In 2040 BC the Middle Kingdom began as a time of stability and growth. (Middle)
3. The New Kingdom, an age ruled by pharaohs and gold, began in 1552 BC (End)

Main Idea #1 - _____
_____

I Beg. A. _____
_____

I Mid. B. _____
_____

Now that the three main ideas are found, the hardest part is over. The students now have a focus for their report and can look for details that are primarily about those three topics. This cuts the amount of researching down dramatically. The example above shows how we narrowed our topic on ancient Egypt to three main ideas. Now we only need to look for details on these three main ideas.

Before moving on to the next step, have the students write their three main ideas again, this time on their three main idea note pages. This will keep their main ideas front and center in their minds as they take notes. Staying focused on these three main ideas is a key component of the research report process. Getting sidetracked is very easy, and having the main idea staring at you is a good way to keep on track. Again, this is a detail lost in the note card process.

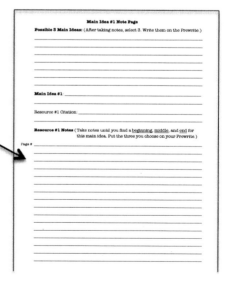

Main Idea #1 Note Page
Possible 3 Main Ideas: (After taking notes, select 3. Write them on the Prewrite.)

Main Idea #1: Egypt's great dynasties began around 3100 B.C. the Old Kingdom.
Resource #1 Citation: _____

Resource #1 Notes (Take notes until you find a beginning, middle, and end for this main idea. Put the three you choose on your Prewrite.)
Page # _____

- - - - - - - - - - - - - - - - - - -

Main Idea #2 Note Page
Main Idea #2: In 2040 B.C. the Middle Kingdom began as a time of stability and growth.
Resource #1: Take notes until you find a beginning, middle, and end for this main idea. Put the three you choose on your Prewrite.)
Page # _____

- - - - - - - - - - - - - - - - - - -

Main Idea #3 Note Page
Main Idea #3: The New Kingdom, an age ruled by pharaohs and gold, began in 1552 B.C.
Resource #1: Take notes until you find a beginning, middle, and end for this main idea. Put the three you choose on your Prewrite.)
Page # _____

Step 5: Take notes from resource #1.

Note: If your students completed the one-paragraph research report, this would be a great time to remind them that they have already done this step before. In that report, they found a beginning, middle, and end for their paragraphs. They are now going to do the exact same thing; only now, they are going to do it three times instead of one.

Now that the students have found their three main ideas, they can start focusing on finding specific details about them. On Main Idea Note Page #1, the students already have a space dedicated for taking notes. As they read through resource #1, remind them that they are only looking for details for that first main idea. Also, because they are only writing one paragraph, they can only find three facts from this resource. If they find more than three, this starts becoming more of a book report than a research report.

Main Idea #1 Note Page
Possible 3 Main Ideas: (After taking notes, select 3. Write them on the Prewrite.)

Main Idea #1: _____

Resource #1 Citation: _____

Resource #1 Notes (Take notes until you find a beginning, middle, and end for this main idea. Put the three you choose on your Prewrite.)
Page # _____

The concept of finding a beginning, middle, and end is one that continues to come up. This is a theme that is easy to remember, which makes it a good strategy for teaching the research report. When the students first start researching a new main idea, looking for a beginning, middle, and end is a great way to begin. Therefore, as you look for main ideas for Main Idea #1, have the students focus on finding a beginning, middle, and end.

The image to the right shows the three facts that we found from resource #1 about our first main idea. The students wrote the word "Page" in the margin to remind them to put the page number where the facts were found. They will need this for the Endnotes section of the report.

7. Egyptian Gods
8. New Kingdom

Main Idea #1: Egypt's great dynasties began around 3100 BC during the Old Kingdom.
Resource #1 Citation: Reflections: Ancient Civilizations (Textbook); Chapter 4, Orlando, Harcourt, 2007
Resource #1 Notes:
Page #
143 The Old Kingdom began with the first dynasty started by King Narmer who united Upper and Lower Egypt.
144 During the Old Kingdome, the ancient Egyptians learned to make mummies because they believed their bodies would be needed in the afterlife.
145 The Old Kingdom is known as the Age of Pyramids because the rulers built them as their tombs.

This is a good time to remind the students about plagiarism. If a student copies from a book into his/her notes, then copies from the notes into the report, the student is still plagiarizing. It is important that the students write their notes in their own words.

Now that the students have their three facts from resource #1, have the students write them on their Prewrite under Main Idea #1. Notice that the worksheet has "I Beg.," "I Mid.," and I End" in the margins. This will remind them that these notes were found in

Research Report Prewrite
3 Main Ideas:
1. Egypt's great dynasties began around 3100 BC during the Old Kingdom.
2. In 2040 BC the Middle Kingdom began as a time of stability and growth.
3. The New Kingdom, an age ruled by pharaohs and gold, began in 1552 BC.
   Main Idea #1 -
   I Beg. A. The Old Kingdom began with the first dynasty started by King Narmer who united Upper and Lower Egypt. P. 143
   I Mid. B. During the Old Kingdom, the ancient Egyptians learned to make mummies because they believed their bodies would be needed in the afterlife. P. 144
   I End C. The Old Kingdom is known as the Age of Pyramids because the rulers built them as their tombs.
   II Sup D.
   Det.
   II Sup E.
   Det.
   III Sup F.
   Det.
   III Sup G.
   Det.

resource #1 (represented by the I) and that each detail represents the beginning (Beg.), the middle (Mid.), and end (End). The students who are creating their own prewrite will need to write these items on their own.

Note: An interesting event occurred as my class was looking through resource #1 on our reports on ancient Egypt. While looking for three details to support the Old Kingdom, we came across a great detail for our third main idea, the New Kingdom. Because we already had our papers set up to accept details for all parts of our essay, we had a place to put this new fact:

"By the time of the New Kingdom, along with the mummified body, the priests would place the Book of the Dead in the tomb. This book explained a 'weighing of the hear' ceremony which decided the fate of their souls."

We were able to add this new detail to the third cluster on resource #1.

Warning: At this point, explaining the process might get confusing. There are two directions we can go from here. First, we can continue finding facts about our first main idea from the second and third resources. The second option is to stick with resource #1 and find details for our second and third main ideas. Since we have our first resource out, sticking with the first resource and finding details on our second and third main ideas is the path we are going to take.

Using resource #1, the students have found the beginning, middle, and end for their first main idea. Next, the students will repeat the same process, still using resource #1 to find the beginning, middle, and end details for the Main Idea #2. They will write their notes on

> *Main Idea #2 Note Page*
> **Main Idea #2**: *In 2040 BC the Middle Kingdom began as a time of stability and growth.*
>
> *Resource #1 Notes*
> *Page #*
> 151 *The rulers of the Middle Kingdom strengthened Egypt by improving forts, irrigation, and temples.*
> 152 *This was a period of heavy trade as Egypt traded its grains, minerals, and precious stones for silver, copper, gold, and incense.*
> 153 *By conquering lower Egypt, the Hyksos brought their better technology into Egyptian society.*

Main Idea #2 Note Page and add their three main ideas to the Prewrite. Again, be sure the students write the page numbers where each detail was found.

They will follow the same procedure again with Main Idea #3 by writing their notes on Main Idea #3 Note Page and adding their three main ideas to the Prewrite. To the right is an image showing what Main Idea #3 Note Page would look like.

Main Idea #3 Note Page

Main Idea #3: The New Kingdom, an age ruled by pharaohs and gold, began in 1552 BC.

Resource #1 Notes:

Page #

159   Hatshepsut, one of the only female pharaohs, invaded Egypt's neighbors, brought back riches, and set up trade.

159   Egypt would gain increased wealth until it began to lose power and land.

146   By the New Kingdom, along with the mummified body, the priests would place the Book of the Dead in the tomb. This book explained the "weighing of the heart" ceremony which decided the fate of their souls.

Below is an image showing the front and back of the prewrite. Remember, the students have only gone through resource #1. This is why each main idea of the prewrite is still incomplete.

Front

Research Report Prewrite

3 Main Ideas:
1. Egypt's great dynasties began around 3100 BC during the Old Kingdom.
2. In 2040 BC the Middle Kingdom began as a time of stability and growth.
3. The New Kingdom, an age ruled by pharaohs and gold, began in 1552 BC.

Main Idea #1 – Egypt's great dynasties began around 3100 BC during the Old Kingdom.

I Beg.   A.   The Old Kingdom began with the first dynasty started by King Narmer who united Upper and Lower Egypt. P. 143

I Mid.   B.   During the Old Kingdom, the ancient Egyptians learned to make mummies because they believed their bodies would be needed in the afterlife. P. 144

I End   C.   The Old Kingdom is known as the Age of Pyramids because the rulers built them as their tombs.

II Sup D.
     Det.
II Sup E.
     Det.
III Sup F.
     Det.
III Sup G.
     Det.

Main Idea #2 – In 2040 BC the Middle Kingdom began as a time of stability and growth.

I Beg.   A.   The rulers of the Middle Kingdom strengthened Egypt by improving forts, irrigation, and temples. P. 151

I Mid.   B.   This was a period of heavy trade as Egypt traded its grains, minerals, and precious stones for silver, copper, gold, and incense. P. 152

I End   C.   By conquering lower Egypt, the Hyksos brought their better technology into Egyptian society. P. 153

Back

Research Report Prewrite

3 Main Ideas:
1. Egypt's great dynasties began around 3100 BC during the Old Kingdom.
2. In 2040 BC the Middle Kingdom began as a time of stability and growth.
3. The New Kingdom, an age ruled by pharaohs and gold, began in 1552 BC.

Main Idea #1 – Egypt's great dynasties began around 3100 BC during the Old Kingdom.

I Beg.   A.   The Old Kingdom began with the first dynasty started by King Narmer who united Upper and Lower Egypt. P. 143

I Mid.   B.   During the Old Kingdom, the ancient Egyptians learned to make mummies because they believed their bodies would be needed in the afterlife. P. 144

I End   C.   The Old Kingdom is known as the Age of Pyramids because the rulers built them as their tombs.

II Sup D.
     Det.
II Sup E.
     Det.
III Sup F.
     Det.
III Sup G.
     Det.

Main Idea #2 – In 2040 BC the Middle Kingdom began as a time of stability and growth.

I Beg.   A.   The rulers of the Middle Kingdom strengthened Egypt by improving forts, irrigation, and temples. P. 151

I Mid.   B.   This was a period of heavy trade as Egypt traded its grains, minerals, and precious stones for silver, copper, gold, and incense. P. 152

I End   C.   By conquering lower Egypt, the Hyksos brought their better technology into Egyptian society. P. 153

Step 6: Take notes from resource #2.

The students are now going to repeat the process from step five for the second resource. They are going to write a few possible details for all three main ideas on all three Main Idea Note Pages #1, #2, and #3. Next, they will decide which two best support the main ideas for the beginning, middle, and end from resource #1. Because these are supporting details, when they write them on their Prewrite, they can write "SD" or "Sup. Det." in the margin next to the detail. Thus, they will have "II SD" next to the two new facts on their Prewrite. See the sample to the right.

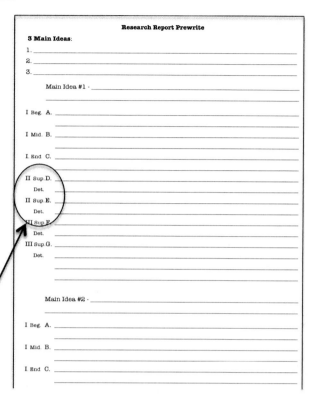

Remember, at this point of the process, the students should be looking for details that will expand on the details found in resource #1. Notice that the *beginning* details of resource #1 were about King Narmer uniting upper and lower Egypt, pyramids, and the afterlife. From our second resource we didn't see any more details about King Narmer. However, we were able to find two facts that added to what we already knew about the afterlife and one fact about what we knew about the pyramids.

This same idea will apply when the students look for supporting details from resource #3. The students would then have two to three more details for all three topics bringing their total of details up to five to six. The sample to the right shows how my class finished this step of the assignment. They found two more details from resource #3 that supported the three main ideas from resource #1. We found more information about King Narmer which will make great supporting details for this paragraph.

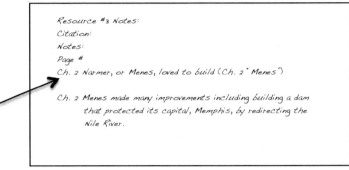

Resource #3 Notes:
Citation:
Notes:
Page #
Ch. 2 Narmer, or Menes, loved to build (Ch. 2 "Menes")

Ch. 2 Menes made many improvements including building a dam that protected its capital, Memphis, by redirecting the Nile River.

Before they move on to resource #3, they still need to find two facts for main ideas #2 and #3. Below are examples of what their prewrite will look like when they complete finding supporting details from resource #2. Notice that the roman number II is now complete for all three main ideas.

Front   Back

Research Report Prewrite

3 Main Ideas:
1. Egypt's great dynasties began around 3100 BC during the Old Kingdom.
2. In 2040 BC the Middle Kingdom began as a time of stability and growth.
3. The New Kingdom, an age ruled by pharaohs and gold, began in 1552 BC.

Main Idea #1 – Egypt's great dynasties began around 3100 BC during the Old Kingdom.

I Beg. A. The Old Kingdom began with the first dynasty started by King Narmer who united Upper and Lower Egypt. P. 143
I Mid. B. During the Old Kingdom, the ancient Egyptians learned to make mummies because they believed their bodies would be needed in the afterlife. P. 144
I End C. The Old Kingdom is known as the Age of Pyramids because the rulers built them as their tombs.
II Sup D. The pyramids were built by the rulers as a home for the Det. afterlife and as a place to be worshipped long after they died.
II Sup E. They believed that the body was needed because this is Det. where the soul, or ka, lived.
III Sup F.
Det.
III Sup G.
Det.

Main Idea #2 – In 2040 BC the Middle Kingdom began as a time of stability and growth.

I Beg. A. The rulers of the Middle Kingdom strengthened Egypt by improving forts, irrigation, and temples. P. 151
I Mid. B. This was a period of heavy trade as Egypt traded its grains, minerals, and precious stones for silver, copper, gold, and incense. P. 152
I End C. By conquering lower Egypt, the Hyksos brought their better technology into Egyptian society. P. 153

Main Idea #2 (Cont.) –

II Sup D. One giant project was an irrigation ditch that created a Det. man-made lake from the Nile that prevented flooding and provided water. P. 34
II Sup E. The wealthy were able to trade for luxuries such as long Det. fabric, heavy bracelets, and necklaces made of gold.
III Sup F.
Det.
III Sup G.
Det.

Main Idea #3 – The New Kingdom, an age ruled by pharaohs and gold, began in 1552 BC.

I Beg. A. Hatshepsut, one of the only female pharaohs, invaded Egypt's neighbors, brought back riches, and set up trade. P. 159
I Mid. B. Egypt would gain increased wealth until it began to lose power and land. P. 159
I End C. By the New Kingdom, along with the mummified body, the priests would place the Book of the Dead in the tomb. This book explained the "weighing of the heart" ceremony which decided the fate of their souls. P. 159
II Sup D. On one of Hatshepsut's most famous trading trips, she Det. returned from eastern Africa with ships full of myrrh, ebony wood, ivory, gold, make up, and a variety of animals. P. 40-41
II Sup E. Pharaohs began building secret tombs due to grave robbing. Det. Hatshepsut built one tomb for show and one for herself. P. 40-41
III Sup F.
Det.
III Sup G.
Det.

Step 7: Take notes from resource #3.

By now, your students have found three facts from resource #1 and two or three facts from resource #2. Because paragraphs are normally no longer than seven sentences, this means that there is not much room for many details from our third source. They will need to be extremely judicious about which facts are relevant from the third source.

Begin by reviewing the details that you already have. Next, search through the third resource for details that would enhance the details you have already found. This would be a good place to find a fun fact or a quote from a primary source that would support each of our main ideas.

As the students find more supporting details, have them write their notes on Main Idea #1 Note Page in the Resource #3 Note section. Make sure the students write the page numbers where they found each detail. Be sure to add these details to the Prewrite. After repeating this process for Main Ideas #2 and #3, you now have a completed prewrite.

Step 8: Organize your notes.

By now, the students have their three topics, up to nine facts about each topic, and the location where these facts were found. All they need to do now is to organize these details into one report.

Organizing the notes on the Prewrite:

The students need to decide the order in which their facts will appear in their paragraphs. The students practiced this when they completed the one-paragraph research report. This time, instead of only doing it once, they will need to do it three times, once for Main Idea #1, once for Main Idea #2, and once for Main Idea #3.

Begin by having the students look at the Main Idea #1 section of their Prewrite. They need to decide the order in which these details will appear in their paragraphs. The students will number these details in the order they should appear in their paragraphs. Keep in mind that they may not be able to use all of their details. Also, they may be able to combine several details into one. The example to the right shows this process for the first main idea of our Egypt report.

Have the students repeat this process again for Main Ideas #2 and #3 on their Prewrite. They will number the details in the order that the details will appear in the paragraphs. All three main idea paragraphs are now organized and ready for the students' rough drafts.

Step 9: Write your introduction paragraph.

Once again, if you used *How to Teach the Five-Paragraph Essay* with your students, you've already taught your students this step. They already know how to write a basic introduction or an interesting introduction based on the notes they've already taken.

If you haven't taught essay introductions, here's an overview of a basic introduction. The students are going to make a thesis statement, tell the three main ideas, and prepare the reader for the essay with a transition sentence that will lead into their first main idea.

The Thesis Statement: In a true thesis statement, a writer will be stating the purpose of the paper. The writer will be making arguments or asserting ideas that will be supported later in the paper. However, we are still in the training-wheel phase of research report writing. For our five-paragraph report, we are just going to ask our students to tell us, in one sentence, the topic of the research report. The students can get as sophisticated as their talents will allow, but they only really need one simple sentence that tells the reader about their report. Here are two examples:

Basic Introduction:
Ancient Egypt was a culture that lasted for thousands of years.

Stronger Introduction:
For thousands of years ancient Egypt would rise and fall creating new ideas and a fascinating culture that is still studied today.

Summarize the Three Main Ideas: On the prewrite of the five-paragraph essay, the students have already written their three main ideas. The students can almost copy them directly into their essay. If they do, they should add transition words to help the sentences flow together. To the right is a copy of the prewrite. The next page shows how the three main ideas are summarized into a basic introduction.

Research Report Prewrite

3 Main Ideas:

1. Egypt's great dynasties began around 3100 BC during the Old Kingdom. (Beginning)
2. In 2040 BC the Middle Kingdom began as a time of stability and growth. (Middle)
3. The New Kingdom, an age ruled by pharaohs and gold, began in 1552 BC (End)

Main Idea #1 - _____

_____

I Beg. A. _____

_____

I Mid. B. _____

_____

Basic Introduction

Ancient Egypt was a culture that lasted for thousands of years. The first of their great dynasties began around 3100 B.C. with the Old Kingdom. In 2040 B.C., the Middle Kingdom began as a time of stability and growth. Finally, in 1552 B.C., the New Kingdom emerged as a period ruled by pharaohs and obsessed with gold. These three kingdoms combined would show how ancient civilizations had many incredible achievements.

Advanced Introduction

For thousands of years ancient Egypt would rise and fall, creating new ideas and a fascinating culture that is still studied today. It began with the Old Kingdom, a time when their culture combined with construction to build magnificent structures. By the Middle Kingdom, Egyptians continued to expand their kingdom using ideas from other lands. Finally, the New Kingdom would be Egypt's time of greatest wealth as strong pharaohs conquered their neighbors. These three kingdoms combined would show how this ancient civilization had many incredible achievements.

Encourage the more advanced students to improve the quality of their sentences rather than simply restating the three main ideas. To the left is an example of an interesting introduction with more sophisticated sentences.

Transition Sentence: This sentence should bring the introduction to a close while preparing the reader for the first main idea. The students tend to overthink this step. Just a simple statement giving an overview would be fine. In our sample introduction, we closed our paragraph with "...combined would show how this ancient civilization had many incredible achievements." Many times, you can borrow words from the last sentence and use them in your topic sentence of the next paragraph to create a smooth transition. In our sample, we can take the words "incredible achievements" and use them in our topic sentence about the Old Kingdom. See the sample to the right.

...combined would show how this ancient civilization had many incredible achievements.

The incredible achievements would begin with the unification of Upper and Lower Egypt...

Step 10: Write the three body paragraphs with endnotes.

The students have now collected their details and have put them in order for all three paragraphs. All they need to do now is use these notes to write their paragraphs. Although they have done this already with the one-paragraph report, they will still need to be shown how to make the notes from the prewriting flow together into smooth paragraphs. Otherwise, their report sounds more like a grocery list of facts rather than one cohesive report.

Below, you can see the prewriting and the first main idea paragraph side by side. Notice that in the paragraph, we were able to use the first detail from our prewrite in our topic sentence. Notice also the transition from the details about Menes to the idea of building pyramids. Again, a great way to make transitions is to borrow words from one idea and use it in the next. We took the word "build" from the sentence on Menes and transitioned to the idea that other pharaohs also built. This allowed us to transition from the idea that Menes built dams and other rulers built pyramids.

Main Idea #1 – Egypt's great dynasties began around 3100 BC during the Old Kingdom.

I Beg. [1] A. The Old Kingdom began with the first dynasty started by King Narmer who united Upper and Lower Egypt. P. 143

I Mid. [6] B. During the Old Kingdom, the ancient Egyptians learned to make mummies because they believed their bodies would be needed in the afterlife. P. 144

I End [4] C. The Old Kingdom is known as the Age of Pyramids because the rulers built them as their tombs.

II Sup Det. [5] D. The pyramids were built by the rulers as a home for the afterlife and as a place to be worshipped long after they died.

II Sup Det. [7] E. They believed that the body was needed because this is where the soul, or ka, lived.

III Sup Det. [2] F. Narmer, or Menes, loved to build. Ch. 2

III Sup Det. [3] G. Menes made many improvements including building a dam that protected its capital by redirecting the Nile River. Ch. 2

Main Idea #2 – In 2040 BC the Middle Kingdom began as a time of stability and growth.

I Beg. A. The rulers of the Middle Kingdom strengthened Egypt by improving forts, irrigation, and temples. P. 151

I Mid. B. This was a period of heavy trade as Egypt traded its grains, minerals, and precious stones for silver, copper, gold, and incense. P. 152

I End C. By conquering lower Egypt, the Hyksos brought their better technology into Egyptian society. P. 153

These incredible achievements would begin with the unification of Upper and Lower Egypt. King Menes would conquer both halves of Egypt and immediately begin to build. He built an incredible dam that changed the course of the Nile River, protected the capital city of Memphis, and provided fresh water for the people. Other rulers would build as well with most of Egypt's many pyramids were built during this time. These pyramids would be a home for their bodies in the afterlife and a way for the rulers to be worshipped long after their death. Besides being great builders of pyramids, they were able to mummify bodies since they believed they would need their bodies to house their soul, or ka. This early time in Egypt's history brought many great achievements to the ancient world.

Citations:

At this point, the students need to decide which facts in their report are worthy of citations. Typically, when using a quote, giving an expert opinion, stating statistics, or writing anything that may require the reader to seek more information about the topic, it needs to be cited. Because this is more of a training exercise, we may not have many of these details in our paragraphs. For this reason, I ask them to find the three most important facts in each paragraph and include a citation for each.

Since the students are citing three facts from each paragraph, they will have nine sentences to document at the end of the report. To cite a key detail, the students will put a 1 in superscript[1] at the end of the sentence. The next citation will have a two[2], the next will have a three[3], and so on. Below is the first body paragraph again, this time with three details given endnote numbers:

These incredible achievements would begin with the unification of Upper and Lower Egypt. King Menes would conquer both halves of Egypt and immediately begin to build. He built an incredible dam that changed the course of the Nile River, protected the capital city of Memphis, and provided fresh water for the people.[1] Other rulers would build as well with most of Egypt's many pyramids being built during this time. These pyramids would be a home for thier bodies in the afterlife and a way for the rulers to be worshipped long after their death.[2] Besides being great builders of pyraids, they were able to mummify bodies since they believed they would need their bodies to house their soul, or ka.[3] This early time in Egypt's history brought many great achievements to the ancient world.

Step 11: Write the conclusion paragraph.

In the conclusion, the students need to summarize their thesis statements, review their main ideas, and give final thoughts on the topic. This can all be easily done by looking back at the prewrite. Follow the steps below and use the sample as a guide for helping your students write a basic conclusion paragraph.

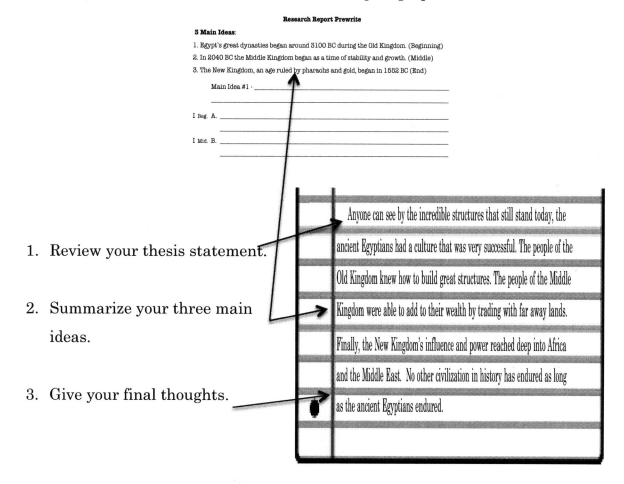

Research Report Prewrite

3 Main Ideas:

1. Egypt's great dynasties began around 3100 BC during the Old Kingdom. (Beginning)
2. In 2040 BC the Middle Kingdom began as a time of stability and growth. (Middle)
3. The New Kingdom, an age ruled by pharaohs and gold, began in 1552 BC (End)

Main Idea #1 - _____

I Beg. A. _____

I Mid. B. _____

1. Review your thesis statement.

2. Summarize your three main ideas.

3. Give your final thoughts.

Anyone can see by the incredible structures that still stand today, the ancient Egyptians had a culture that was very successful. The people of the Old Kingdom knew how to build great structures. The people of the Middle Kingdom were able to add to their wealth by trading with far away lands. Finally, the New Kingdom's influence and power reached deep into Africa and the Middle East. No other civilization in history has endured as long as the ancient Egyptians endured.

Step 12: Make the endnotes and bibliography.

After the conclusion of the report, the students will type "Endnotes" as a heading and list the sources for all endnotes in the order they appeared in the report. For the endnotes, the students need to include the book title, author, publisher, city of publication, the edition (if listed), and the page where the information was found. Since the students already labeled where each fact was found, and all this information is on the top of their notes already, all they need to do is look back at their notes to find which of the three sources had each detail. The next few pages will show how the endnotes will be listed in the report.

Finally, the bibliography is easy. For each book used in the report, the students simply need to copy the same information from the endnotes. However, they can leave out the page numbers.

Below is a sample of the entire report and how the endnotes/bibliography were listed:

For thousands of years ancient Egypt would rise and fall, creating new ideas and a fascinating culture that is still studied today. It began with the Old Kingdom, a time where their culture combined with construction to build magnificent structures. By the Middle Kingdom, Egyptians continued to expand their kingdom using ideas from other lands. Finally, the New Kingdom would be Egypt's time of greatest wealth as strong pharaohs conquered their neighbors. These three kingdoms combined would show how ancient civilization had many incredible achievements.

These incredible achievements would begin with the unification of Upper and Lower Egypt. King Menes would conquer both halves of Egypt and immediately begin to build. He built an incredible dam that changed the course of the Nile River, protected the capital city of Memphis, and provided fresh water for the people.[1] Other rulers would build as well, with most of Egypt's many pyramids built during this time. These pyramids would be a home for their bodies in the afterlife and a way for the rulers to be worshipped long after their deaths.[2] Besides being great builders of pyramids, they were able to mummify bodies since they believed they would need their bodies to house their soul, or ka.[3] This early time in Egypt's history brought many great achievements to the ancient world.

More great achievements would come in the Middle Kingdom. These rulers would build forts, better irrigation, and larger temples across Egypt. One impressive project was an irrigation ditch that created a man-made lake that prevented the Nile from flooding and provided fresh water for the people.[4] A ruler named Sesostris III would build forts along his conquered lands to protect the land and its gold for the kingdom. Besides building, the Middle Kingdom was known for its trade. Egypt would trade its grains, minerals, and precious stones for silver, copper, gold, and incense.[5] The wealthy were able to trade for other luxurious items such as long fabric, heavy bracelets, and necklaces made of gold. Finally, the New Kingdom was able to bring new ideas not only from trade, but also from the people that invaded it. The Hyksos showed the Egyptians how to make chariots and other weapons of war.[6] Although Egypt was able to improve on its achievements from the Old Kingdom, the best was yet to come.

The New Kingdom was the time of Egypt's greatest wealth. One pharaoh who added to its wealth was Hatshepsut, one of the only female pharaohs. She was known to bring ships filled with myrrh, ebony wood, ivory, gold, makeup, and a variety of animals.[7] Hatshepsut and many of the other New Kingdom pharaohs would use the military skills learned from the Hyksos to add even more wealth to Egypt. As great as these pharaohs were, Ramses the Great was the "most magnificent of them all."[8] Using the famous Hyksos chariot and double bow, Ramses expanded Egypt's borders well into the Middle East. By this time, most pharaohs were building secret tombs due to grave robbers. Hatshepsut even built one to present to the people while keeping a secret one for her real tomb. In the New Kingdom, pharaohs weren't the only ones with afterlife privileges. The wealthy were able to be mummified and fill their tombs with treasures.[9] All this wealth, from the pharaohs to the people would be a symbol of Egypt's greatness for hundreds of years.

Anyone can see by the incredible structures that still stand today, the ancient Egyptians had a culture that was very successful. The people of the Old Kingdom knew how to build great structures. The people of the Middle Kingdom were able to add to their wealth by trading with faraway lands. Finally, the New Kingdom's influence and power reached deep into Africa and the Middle East. No other civilization in history has endured as long as the ancient Egyptians endured.

Endnotes

1. Engineering an Empire (History Channel DVD) Chapter 2 "Menes"
2. Reflections: Ancient Civilizations Unit 2 (Orlando: Harcourt, 2007) Pg. 145

3. Hotle, Patrick ,PhD <u>Egypt and the Middle East: Ancient to Present</u> (Mark Twain Media, Inc., 1995) Pg. 22

4. Hotle, Patrick, PhD <u>Egypt and the Middle East: Ancient to Present</u> (Mark Twain Media, Inc., 1995) Pg. 35

5. <u>Reflections: Ancient Civilizations</u> Unit 2 (Orlando: Harcourt, 2007) Pg. 145

6. Hotle, Patrick, PhD <u>Egypt and the Middle East: Ancient to Present</u> (Mark Twain Media, Inc., 1995) Pg. 35

7. Hotle, Patrick, PhD <u>Egypt and the Middle East: Ancient to Present</u> (Mark Twain Media, Inc., 1995) Pg. 40-41

8. <u>Engineering an Empire</u> (History Channel DVD) Chapter 10 "Ramses II"

9. <u>Reflections: Ancient Civilizations</u> Unit 2 (Orlando: Harcourt, 2007) Pg. 159

Bibliography

1. <u>Reflections: Ancient Civilizations</u> Unit 2 (Orlando: Harcourt, 2007)

2. Hotle, Patrick, PhD <u>Egypt and the Middle East: Ancient to Present</u> (Mark Twain Media, Inc., 1995)

3. <u>Engineering an Empire</u> (History Channel DVD)

Conclusion

All that is left is to revise, edit and publish. Although your goal is to teach the students to write research reports on their own, it would be helpful to give students a written copy of the assignment with a checklist of steps to follow and samples of how to format a report. These are items even college professors provide. The appendix has sample assignments for you to use as a guide.

After modeling the five-paragraph research report, give your students the opportunity to practice it on their own. Give them other topics from your curriculum for them to try on their own. They should be able to complete each one in about two weeks, even less if you give them time in class to work on it. The appendix has a generic assignment sheet you can give your students to help them complete a five-paragraph research report. Once your students have mastered this skill, they are amazingly close to knowing how to write a three to five-page research report.

Part III
The Three- to Five-Page Research Report

If the students have mastered the five-paragraph research report, the hard work is mainly finished. Actually writing a three-to-five page research report is surprisingly easy. Rather than writing one five-paragraph essay on one topic, they will basically be writing three or more five-paragraph essays on one topic. The only new aspect to this larger assignment is changing the introduction paragraphs so they become transition paragraphs between each main idea.

Here is an overview of what they already know how to do and what they will be asked to do in this section:

1. They know how to find a beginning, middle, and end for their topic.
   Five-Paragraph Essay: The students will turn the beginning, middle and end into paragraphs.
   Three- to Five-Page Research Report: The students will turn the beginning, middle and end into essays. Another approach would be to find three or for main ideas and

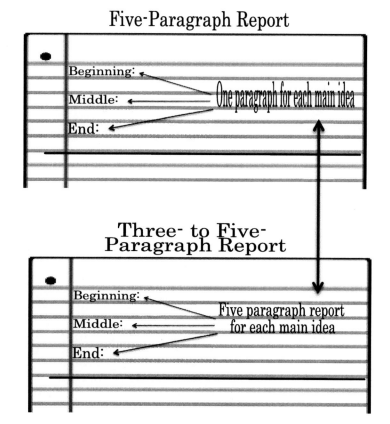

write an essay for each of these. Either way, the concept is the same; think of three or four main ideas and write an essay on each.

Think of it this way. When writing the five-paragraph report, the students found three main ideas and turned each main idea into a paragraph. For the three- to five-page research report, they will turn each main idea into its own five-paragraph essay. By adding an introduction and conclusion paragraph to the three essays, the report should easily make up three pages.

2. Note Taking: The students know how to set up their papers to begin collecting facts. **Five-Paragraph Essay**: The students will set up three pieces of paper by preparing one page for each resource. They will prepare to list the facts for the beginning, middle, and end for each resource on one piece of paper.

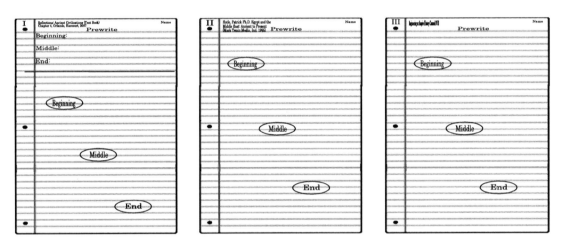

Three- to Five-Page Research Report: The students will set up three pieces of paper to receive the facts for the beginning, middle and end of the essays. They will list their facts from all three resources on the three separate pages. Each page becomes a prewrite for a third of the report.

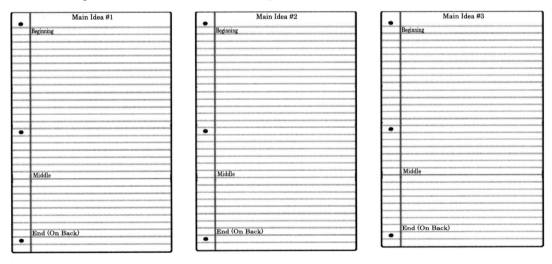

The Steps:

Many teachers assign research reports and expect their students to complete most of the work on their own. The teachers may give some time for research in class, and they may check the students' progress along the way. However, in most cases, the students are expected to do the bulk of the work on their own.

The purpose of this resource is to help guide your students through the process of research report writing. The goal is to create students who are confident writers and are prepared for higher education. The first two-thirds of the book were written as lesson plans for the teacher. The research report was broken into small chunks (one-paragraph and five-paragraph reports) to allow the teacher to model and guide the students through the process.

To foster independence, this section will be written with the students in mind. The teacher can print copies of these pages and use it as an introduction lesson for the report. The students should already be familiar with the steps. Therefore, if the teacher reviews the pages with the students, helps them set up their papers for note taking, and reviews the steps for transition writing, the students should be able to complete the rest of the report on their own.

Teachers of high school students many not have the time to go through this entire book. These teachers can still offer the benefits of the program by spending a couple of days reviewing the one paragraph research report and a couple more on the five-paragraph report. This will still serve as an excellent introduction and confidence builder to the lengthy multiple-page research report.

The Research Report
(Three to Five Pages)

Directions: Follow the steps below to help you write your research report. Check off each step as you complete it.

_____

My Research Report Topic

1. Gather at least three resources for your topic. Two sources must be a hard source such as a book, magazine, or newspaper. One resource can be a soft source such as an Internet website, video, or CD-ROM.

2. Set up your paper for your notes:

   A. 1st Sheet of Paper: Title this page "Bibliography." In the middle of the paper, write "Common Themes/Possible Main Ideas."

   *On this page, make a list of all the resources you use for your report. For each resource, write the book title, author, publisher, city of publication, and the edition (if listed).

   Example:

   1. Carpenter, Allan. <u>The Enchantment of South America: Chile</u>. Chicago: Children's Press, 1969

   **In the middle section and the back of the page, make a list of common ideas that you find as you begin to read through your resources. You should also be looking for a possible beginning, middle, and end for your report.

   B. 2nd, 3rd, and 4th Sheets of Paper: You will read about your topic until you can divide it into three or four main ideas. For these next three sheets of paper (a fourth sheet will be needed if you are using four main ideas) you will write "Main Idea #1," "Main Idea #2", and "Main Idea #3" on the top. You will then write your topics below. For example, a topic on Ancient Rome may have three main ideas such as The Republic, The Empire, The Breakup and Fall. Your three papers would look like this:

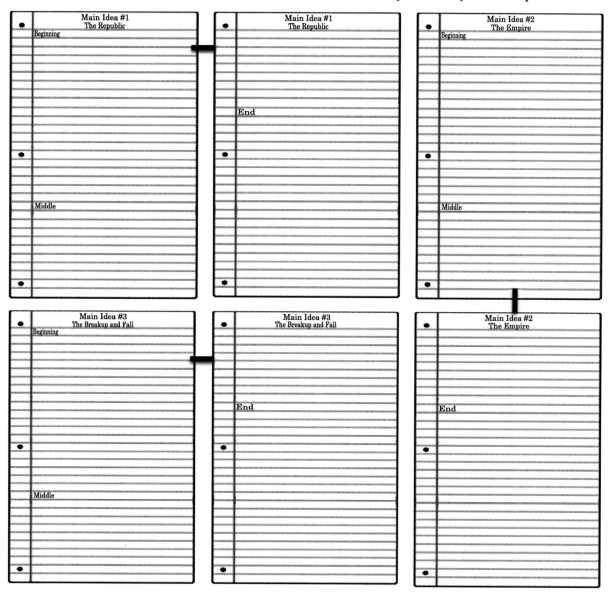

C. Finish Paper Setup: On the first line of your paper, write "Beginning."
About two thirds of the way down, write "Middle," and on the back, about one third of the way down, write "End." Repeat this process for all of your note pages for "Main Idea #2", "Main Idea #3," and "Main Idea #4" (if needed). See sample:

3. Take notes from Resource #1: Search for facts only on you main idea topics. When you find a key detail on any of your topics, put it on the appropriate paper, in the appropriate sections - either the beginning, middle, and end. <u>Don't forget to put the page number where the detail was found</u>. Also, put a roman numeral I in the margin next to each fact you find. This will help you identify that this fact was found in resource #1.

Example: Let's say that in resource #1, you find a good fact about the five good Roman emperors. You already have a place to put this fact. On the Main Idea #2 prewrite, you can place this fact in the "Middle" section of the paper (see example). You now also have an idea of what to look for to add details to the middle section of Main Idea #2. Adding details about these five good emperors is the next logical step.

After reading through resource #1, you may have found details for all the beginnings, middles, and ends for all of your topics, or you may have only found details for some of your main ideas. You will need to find details from as many sources as it takes until you have at least five details for every beginning, middle, and end.

If you aren't sure where a detail belongs in your prewrites, just put it in the section that makes the most sense at the time. As your report begins to take shape, you may see that some details fit better in other sections of your report.

Example: Let's say that you find the following detail about a report about Rome:
"In 285, Emperor <u>Diocletian</u> divided the Roman Empire's administration into eastern and western halves."

This detail would fit well under the notes for "Main Idea #3" under the "Beginning" heading. Later you might find that this detail fits better under the "Middle," but the beginning is a good place to put this fact until more details are found.

66

Continue to take notes from resource #1 until you have found as many relevant details as possible. Remember to write the page numbers for the details and a roman numeral I next to each fact.

4. Take notes from resources #2, #3, and so on: Repeat the note-taking process with resources #2, #3, and beyond until you can explain the beginning, middle, and end of all your topics. Put roman numerals for each resource (roman numeral II for the second resource, roman numeral III for the third resource, and so on.) Also, keep writing the page numbers where the details are found.

   As you take notes, continue to look for good quotes, charts, and images that will enhance your report. Firsthand accounts from people who were experiencing your topic add credibility to your report. Also, as you take notes, you can also start forming opinions about the people and events of your topic. Many teachers and college professors will want you to form an opinion about your topic and use your research to defend it. Opinions are fine (unless otherwise stated by the instructor) as long as you can back them up with facts.

5. Writing your report – The Introduction: Your introduction needs to have two parts. First, you need to have a thesis statement. Next, you need to give a general overview you're your topic.

   Thesis Statement: This is the central idea of your paper. The purpose of your research report is not just summarizing a topic. You are going to make an argument about some aspect of the topic.

   There are several ways to generate a thesis statement. First, if your instructor assigns the topic, simply restate the topic as a question. For example, if the topic is "Write a report about the importance of leadership and cooperation in government through using the rise and fall of the Roman Empire as your model," your thesis statement could then become:

"How does the rise and fall of Rome show the importance of leadership and cooperation within governments?"

If your topic is not assigned, you will need to generate a question or central idea on your own. A good way to do this is to form a basic opinion about your topic that can be your central focus of the paper. Does your topic have a lasting impact today? Did it change the world? Is it something we can learn from today? Did it change how something functions? Basically, come up with a question that can be your major theme or argument that you can make while giving your report The following example shows a basic opinion that is easily defended:

"Rome's innovative governmental structure allowed it to rise and prosper before breaking down and causing it to fall."

General Overview: Many writers will give an overview of their report first, followed by their thesis statement. Others will write the thesis statement first followed by the overview. Both of these styles are acceptable. The primary goal of the overview is to introduce the main ideas of the topic. The secondary goal is to make it as interesting as possible.

There are several techniques that can help make the report interesting. The author can tell a short story that illustrates the thesis statement. For example, beginning an essay about the murder of Julius Caesar would lead right into a thesis statement about leadership and cooperation being important in government. The author could also begin with a quote or offer a statistic that illustrates their thesis.

However you choose to do your introduction, remember these details:
1. Keep it under three paragraphs.
2. Review the main ideas. These are the ideas that you broke into "Beginning," "Middle," and "End" in your note taking.
3. Offer your thesis statement.

6. Writing your report – The Body: You have your thesis statement, your main ideas are organized, and you have the details you need to write your report. Keep these details in mind as you write:

    a. Remember your thesis statement as you write. Write it on an index card and keep it within sight as you write. This will help you stay focused throughout the report.

    b. Any major detail or when you are quoting/citing someone's opinion should have an endnote in subscript.[1] When adding these endnotes to your report, also put the number of the endnote in your notes. Use a highlighter to make it stand out. This will make it easier to list your endnotes when the time comes.

    c. Look for places in your report to add visuals, images, or charts to help illustrate your ideas. Be sure to document these items with endnotes.

7. Writing your report – The Conclusion: The conclusion is going to be very similar to your introduction. You will summarize your thesis statement and review your main ideas. Finally, you will end your report with any final thoughts that bring your report to a close. These final thoughts might include details about how your topic is relevant today. It could show your topic's impact on the world or how it compares to other noteworthy topics. However you write your conclusion, keep it to one to three paragraphs.

8. Revise and edit your report: Read through your report. Are there any weak areas of your report? Are there any ideas that need to be supported with more information? Go through your report. Have someone else look through your report. Look for any issues that need to be addressed including spelling, grammar, and punctuation.

9. Type your report: Most instructors will give you guidelines for your final draft. These may include font size and style, how wide the margins should be, and the need for cover pages, footnotes or endnotes, and bibliography.

Unless specifically stated by the instructor, these are general guidelines for the final draft of your research report:

1. One-inch margins on all sides.
2. Twelve-point font, double spaced.
3. Page numbers on the bottom center.
4. <u>Without Title Page</u>: In the upper left corner of the first page, put your name, the teacher's name, subject or course name, and the date. Double space and put the title of the report, centered. Finally, double space again and begin typing your report.

    <u>With Title Page</u>: Type your thesis statement centered near the top of the paper. Put your name, the teacher's name, subject or course name, and the date in the lower right corner.
5. **Endnotes**: Make a heading at the end of your report for "Endnotes." List the endnotes in the order they appear in your report with the following information: the book title, author, publisher, city of publication, year of publication, the edition, and the page number.

    Example:

    Endnotes

    1. <u>Engineering an Empire</u> (History Channel DVD) Chapter 2 "Menes"
    2. <u>Reflections: Ancient Civilizations</u> Unit 2 (Orlando: Harcourt, 2007) Pg. 145
    3. Hotle, Patrick, PhD <u>Egypt and the Middle East: Ancient to Present</u> (Mark Twain Media, Inc., 1995) Pg. 22

6. **Bibliography**: Make a list of your resources. Include the same information as the endnote except for the page numbers. Example:

    Bibliography

    1. <u>Reflections: Ancient Civilizations</u> Unit 2 (Orlando: Harcourt ,2007)
    2. Hotle, Patrick, PhD <u>Egypt and the Middle East: Ancient to Present</u> (Mark Twain Media, Inc., 1995)

3. <u>Engineering an Empire</u> (History Channel DVD)

4. Chile: http://www.odci.gov/ca/publications/factbook/geos/ci.html

10. Turning in your report: Again, most teachers will tell you specifically how they want your final product turned in. Some teachers simply ask for a staple in the left-hand corner, while others ask for the report in a bound cover complete with a typed table of contents. Some teachers even ask for your notes to help verify that the report was your original work. However your instructor asks for the final draft, be sure to save your notes until you have the final grade.

Appendices

Directions for Bibliography
(See example)

Put your source information in this order:

    1. Alphabetize by author   (last name, first name)

    2. Title of book, article, CD, http://, etc.

    3. Place of publication

    4. Year of publication

    5. Volume and page numbers

Examples:

Carpenter, Allan. The Enchantment of South America: Chile. Chicago: Children's Press, 1969

Microsoft Encyclopedia, 2009 ed., "Chile"

World Book Encyclopedia, 1986, "Chile," pgs. 366-372

Chile:

http://www.odci.gov/ca/publications/factbook/geos/ci.html

American Revolution
Mini Research Reports

Use the information below to find four to five facts about each event. Find two more facts on your own using the Internet or books to complete your prewriting.

1. The French and Indian War: Worksheet Pg. 37 / Textbook Pgs. 320 – 321.
2. The Stamp and Townshend Acts – Printout / Textbook Pg. 330
3. The Boston Massacre – Story Telling Notes and Quiz / Textbook Pgs. 331 – 332.
4. The Boston Tea Party and the Coercive Acts – Worksheet Pg. 48 / Textbook Pgs. 337 – 338.
5. 1st and 2nd Continental Congress – Printout / Worksheet Pg. 50 / Textbook Pgs. 339, 343
6. The Battle of Lexington and Concord - Worksheet Pg. 49 / Textbook Pg. 340

Prewriting Setup

1. _____

The
French and Indian
War

Final Drafts

Write your rough drafts on the bottom half of your paper.

The Five-Paragraph Essay
Research Report

Directions: Follow the steps below to help you write your research report. Check off each step as you complete it.

_____

My Research Report Topic

_____ 1. Gather three resources for your topic. Two sources must be a hard source such as a book, magazine, or newspaper. One resource can be a soft source such as an Internet website, video, or CD-ROM.

_____ 2. Setup for Notes

*If using the premade worksheets, skip to Step 5:

1. **1st Sheet of Paper**: Write "Main Idea #1 Note Page" on the top center. Write "Possible 3 Main Ideas" on the first line. Skip eight lines and write "Main Idea #1." Skip two lines and write "Resource #1 Citation." Skip two lines and write "Resource #1 Notes" and below that write "Page #" in the margin. On the back of this paper, write "Resource #2 Notes," "Citation" on the line below, and "Page #" in the margin. Finally, in the middle of the page, write "Resource #3 Notes," "Citation," and "Page #" in the margin.

2. **2nd Sheet of Paper**: Write "Main Idea #2 Note Page" in the top center of the paper. Write "Main Idea #2:" on the first line. Skip two lines and write "Resource #1 Notes." On the back of the paper, have the students write "Resource #2 Notes" on the top line and "Resource #3 Notes" about half way down the paper.

3. **3rd Sheet of Paper**: Repeat Step 2. Put #3 rather than the #2 to represent Main Idea #3.

4. **4th Sheet of Paper**: For the outline of your report, write "Research Report Prewrite" in the top center of the paper. On the first line, write "3 Main Ideas:" on the first line followed by the numbers 1, 2, and 3 on the next three lines (one on each line.) On the next line, write "Main Idea #1." Skip lines as

you write A, B, C, and so on until you reach G. Repeat this process again for Main Idea #2 and Main Idea #3 continuing on the back of the paper.

5. On Main Idea #1 Note Page, write the citation information for your three resources next to "Citation" below each main idea.

Citation
1. Author of resource
2. Book, magazine, Internet site, or title of resource such as CD or movie title.
3. Article title or chapter (if relevant)
4. City of publication (list only the first city.)
5. Publisher and year of publication
6. Edition of the publication (if any)
• Videos, Internet articles, and other sources may not list some of this information. Simply list what you can find.

_____ 3. Review your topic. Read through your three resources.

_____ 4. Find your three main ideas. Read through resource #1, and make a list of several main ideas on Main Idea #1 Note Page below "Possible Main Ideas." Your goal is to find a beginning, middle, and end for your report. Once you have found three strong main ideas write them on your Research Report Prewrite. Write each main idea next to the 1, 2, and 3.

_____ 5. Still from resource #1, find three (3) facts (a beginning, middle, and end) for Main Idea #1. Write possible details below "Main Idea #1 Notes." Select the three best and write them on your Research Report Prewrite next to A, B, and C below Main Idea #1.

Repeat this process from resource #1 again for Main Idea #2 and Main Idea #3. Write your notes on the note pages and the final details on the prewrite.

_____ 6. From resource #2, find two or three (2-3) facts that are supporting details for the beginning, middle, and end for Main Idea #1. Write possible details on Main Idea #1 Note Page under "Resource #2." Select the two best and write them on your prewrite next to D and E.

Repeat this process from resource #2 again for Main Idea #2 and Main Idea #3. Write your notes on the note pages and the final details on the prewrite.

_____ 7. From resource #3, find one or two (1-2) facts that are supporting details for the fact already found for Main Idea #1. Write possible details on Main Idea #1 Note Page under "Resource #3." Select the one or two best and write them on your prewrite next to F and G.

Repeat this process from resource #3 again for Main Idea #2 and Main Idea #3. Write your notes on the note pages and the final details on the prewrite.

_____ 8. Organize the notes in your prewrite. Look at the notes on your prewrite for Main Idea #1. Decide on the order that these details will appear in the paragraph and number them accordingly. Repeat this for the notes in Main Idea #2 and Main Idea #3.

_____ 9. Write your report. Include an introduction paragraph, three body paragraphs, and a conclusion paragraph. Make two citations for each paragraph in the body.

_____ 10. Write your endnotes and bibliography. Below is a sample of each.

Endnotes

1. <u>Engineering an Empire</u> (History Channel DVD) Chapter 2 "Menes"
2. <u>Reflections: Ancient Civilizations</u> Unit 2 (Orlando: Harcourt, 2007) Pg. 145
3. Hotle, Patrick Ph.D. <u>Egypt and the Middle East: Ancient to Present</u> (Mark Twain Media, Inc., 1995) Pg. 22

Bibliography

1. <u>Reflections: Ancient Civilizations</u> Unit 2 (Orlando: Harcourt, 2007)
2. Hotle, Patrick, PhD <u>Egypt and the Middle East: Ancient to Present</u> (Mark Twain Media, Inc., 1995)
3. <u>Engineering an Empire</u> (History Channel DVD)

_____ 11. Revise and edit your rough draft. Check your report for spelling and punctuation. Also, check for any parts of your report that need clarification or rewording.

_____ 12. Type your final draft.

Main Idea #1 Note Page

Possible 3 Main Ideas: (After taking notes, select 3. Write them on the Prewrite.)

_____

_____

_____

_____

_____

_____

_____

Main Idea #1: _____

_____

Resource #1 Citation: _____

_____

Resource #1 Notes (Take notes until you find a <u>beginning</u>, <u>middle</u>, and <u>end</u> for this main idea. Put the 3 you choose on your Prewrite.)

Page #

_____

_____

_____

_____

_____

_____

_____

_____

_____

_____

_____

_____

_____

Resource #2 Notes:

Citation: _____

_____

Notes (Take notes until you find 2 details that support the 3 main ideas from resource #1. Put the notes you choose on your Prewrite.)

Page #

_____
_____
_____
_____
_____
_____
_____
_____
_____
_____
_____

Resource #3 Notes:

Citation: _____

_____

(Take notes until you find 1 or 2 details that support the main ideas from resource #1 and #2. Put the notes you choose on your Prewrite.)

Page #

_____
_____
_____
_____
_____
_____
_____
_____
_____
_____

Main Idea #2: _____

_____

Resource #1: (Take notes until you find a <u>beginning</u>, <u>middle</u>, and <u>end</u> for this main idea. Put the 3 you choose on your Prewrite.)

Page #

_____

_____

_____

_____

_____

_____

_____

_____

_____

_____

_____

_____

_____

_____

_____

_____

_____

_____

_____

_____

_____

_____

_____

Resource #2:

(Take notes until you <u>find 2 details</u> that support the 3 main ideas from resource #1. Put the notes you choose on your Prewrite.)

Page #

_____

_____

_____

_____

_____

_____

_____

_____

_____

_____

Resource #3:

(Take notes until you <u>find 1 or 2 details</u> that support the main ideas from resource #1 and #2. Put the notes you choose on your Prewrite.)

Page #

_____

_____

_____

_____

_____

_____

_____

_____

_____

_____

_____

Main Idea #3: _____

_____

Resource #1: (Take notes until you find a <u>beginning</u>, <u>middle</u>, and <u>end</u> for this main idea. Put the three you choose on your Prewrite.)

Page #

_____

_____

_____

_____

_____

_____

_____

_____

_____

_____

_____

_____

_____

_____

_____

_____

_____

_____

_____

_____

_____

_____

Resource #2:

(Take notes until you <u>find 2 details</u> that support the 3 main ideas from resource #1. Put the notes you choose on your Prewrite.)

Page #

_____

_____

_____

_____

_____

_____

_____

_____

_____

_____

_____

Resource #3:

(Take notes until you <u>find 1 or 2 details</u> that support the main ideas from resource #1 and #2. Put the notes you choose on your Prewrite.)

Page #

_____

_____

_____

_____

_____

_____

_____

_____

_____

_____

Research Report Prewrite

3 Main Ideas:

1. _____

2. _____

3. _____

Main Idea #1 - _____

_____

I Beg. A. _____

_____

I Mid. B. _____

_____

I. End C. _____

_____

II Sup.D. _____

Det. _____

II Sup.E. _____

Det. _____

III Sup.F. _____

Det. _____

III Sup.G. _____

Det. _____

_____

_____

Main Idea #2 _____

_____

I Beg. A. _____

_____

I Mid. B. _____

_____

I. End C. _____

_____

II Sup. D. _____

    Det. _____

II Sup. E. _____

    Det. _____

III Sup. F. _____

    Det. _____

III Sup. G. _____

    Det. _____

_____

_____

_____

Main Idea #3 - _____

_____

I Beg. A. _____

_____

I Mid. B. _____

_____

I. End C. _____

_____

II Sup. D. _____

    Det. _____

II Sup. E. _____

    Det. _____

III Sup. F. _____

    Det. _____

III Sup. G. _____

    Det. _____

_____

_____